Book Publishing Secrets

A Step-by-Step Guide To Self-Publishing Your Book on Amazon & Profiting From It

Jason Johns

If you have enjoyed this book, please leave a review on Amazon. I read each review personally and the feedback helps me to continually improve my books.

As someone who has bought this book on Amazon you are entitled to a free download of the Kindle version. This will enable you to get the full color book in electronic format. Unfortunately I have to publish these books in black and white in order to make them affordable due to the high cost of color printing. Please download this from Amazon; you can read it on a Kindle or any tablet, cell phone or computer with the free Kindle Reader installed from your app store.

TABLE OF CONTENTS

WHY WRITE & PUBLISH BOOKS

Many claim that the book industry is dead, or at the very least dying, yet people still buy millions and millions of books every single year. But people aren't just buying electronic books; people are buying physical books too. Although book shops are getting scarcer, the market is moving away from e-books and back towards printed books.

Why? Industry experts aren't sure, but they suspect it is because people spend so much time in front of electronic screens that they want a break and a physical book is an ideal escape. It doesn't run out of battery, is immune to screen glare and there is something very satisfying about holding a real book.

However, sales patterns are interesting. In 2016, the book market was worth £3.5 billion ($4.5 billion) in the United Kingdom alone, even though e-book sales dropped by 3%. The biggest increase in the UK was in children's books; sales increased by a massive 16%, making it a great market to be in. The nonfiction market, and in particular self-help, increased by 9% in 2016, while fiction saw a surprising drop in sales of 7%.

So, industry figures show that the publishing industry is alive and well, with sales of children's books increasing significantly as well as sales of nonfiction. What is interesting is that a significant proportion of those sales are not traditional published books, but books published by indie authors, such as you and I. Indie authors are grabbing a significant market share, with many authors who are unhappy with traditional publishing contracts self-publishing their books using these techniques. Through this, they are building a significant income and fan base without the limitations of a traditional publisher.

Anyone can write a book, and it is a fantastic way for you to make money to earn a living. In today's culture of minimum wage and uncertain job security, having a backup plan is more important than ever. Having your own publishing empire provides you with additional income that can be turned into a full-time income if you want.

Publishing has a lot of benefits to you, including:

- Work from anywhere – as a writer you can work from anywhere in the world! I know people who have moved to exotic countries because of the nice weather and cheap cost of living. Personally, I work anywhere and everywhere with my portable "office," I sit working while waiting in the hospital for appointments and am writing this sat in a supermarket café waiting for my son to finish some extra schooling.

- Work at times that suit you – writers can work the hours that they find best for them. Not a morning person? Write at night! I write for a couple of hours in the morning before the children get up, then while they are at school and again in the evening when they are in bed. I write less in the school holidays because I am taking the kids out on adventures.

- Passive income – when we're out on our adventures during school holidays I am still earning money! Recently there was a two week period where I was unable to do any work at all, yet I still earned money. As a self-published author you are earning money whether or not you work, so long as your books continue to sell, which they will if you set up your system properly.

- Minimal start-up costs – it is possible to start this business with zero investment. Most people will have access to a computer they can write on. Self-publishing doesn't cost a penny, and all you need to buy is a cover, but if you or a friend have any artistic talents then you can design your own cover and not spend any money at all! The cost to me of publishing my first book was $5, and it made that back in the first few days.

- Compatible with existing job – if you already have a job then writing is completely compatible with it. You can write before or after work, on the weekends or even at lunchtime. Many authors start their writing career while in a full-time job and leave their job to focus on their writing when they have built up enough of an income. This approach is very beneficial as it takes away much of the pressure for the writing career to produce income and you can progress at a more reasonable pace.

I started writing after my son was diagnosed with leukemia. Both myself and my wife were working, but when he was rushed into hospital everything changed, and we ended up having to quit our jobs to avoid the risk of infection and to care for him. The problem was when we stopped working, the pay checks stopped coming too.

Unfortunately, being at the wrong age and having a son with a critical illness, we were untouchable as far as employers were concerned. We were both over qualified, had been out of work too long or they were concerned about the effect our son's illness would have on our ability to work.

We needed income and, having spent a lot of time writing reports and instruction manuals in my day job, I decided that I could translate that into writing books. I started my first book on a game called Minecraft, which my son had become obsessed with in the hospital. I published it on a shoestring budget (I spent a total of $5 on the entire project), and it started making sales … a lot of sales.

I was instantly hooked and started writing more books. Sadly, as far as Minecraft was concerned, a major software company bought the game and immediately stopped all books produced by independent writers from being published.

However, by that time I had branched into other niches and was writing books on different subjects and I saw a regular income. The nice thing about it was I could work around my son's illness. When he was sick, I could look after him and then write when he was asleep or well. I could work from an old laptop that (just about) ran Microsoft Word. I was earning money literally without spending any, making it ideal for our situation.

Now our son has recovered fully, and I did attempt to get a "proper" job but found no one would employ me with a two-year gap in my resume. Not even able to get a job packing bags at my local supermarket, I turned back to publishing, applied for a business loan to get the equipment I needed and worked to turn it into a full-time income. Sure, it was hard work initially, but the work has paid off as the income increased month on month and my earnings were compounded by books I had previously published. It took about a year from me making this decision for it to become a comfortable full-time income.

You can see from my story that writing can be a success and a potential life changer, and it can be for any one. You too can replicate this success and build the income you want from publishing.

Anyone Can Become An Author

Right now you may be wondering how you are ever going to write a book, but take a deep breath and calm down, I will show you exactly how you can write your own books, whether you want to publish children's books, fiction books or nonfiction books. Most of the focus of this book will be nonfiction, purely because it is easier to get an income from, easier to start up and requires less promotion to see sales. We will also be focusing on Amazon as a platform for selling your books, but there are other marketplaces out there which we will discuss, and I'll show you how to utilize them.

As you read this book, I will show you exactly how to come up with great ideas for books that are in profitable niches, how to find excellent content and how to ensure your books are well received.

I will say straight up though, that your book has to be high quality for it to succeed. Time and time again I see people produce poor quality, badly written books and then wonder why they do not sell online. They won't sell because people won't pay for trash! Amazon are cracking down on poorly written books, so you need to make sure your book reads well, which I will show you how to do.

Your books also need to be a reasonable length, which is something many people 'forget' to teach their students. There are too many people being taught that writing a book that is between 6,000 and 12,000 words is acceptable and then to charge $2.99 to $4.99 for the Kindle version and over $13 for the printed version. Sure, you make a lot of money for each sale, but you have to work hard to get that sale, and your books certainly do not sell themselves.

In my experience, the minimum book length should be 20,000, though if it can be longer, it should be. Particularly with nonfiction, lengths of between 20,000 and 50,000 works well, though if you are going over that, then you can look at splitting your book into two. One can be a permanently free book used to make additional sales, if you have a series, or they can both be paid for books.

You may think this a lot of words, but it isn't as many as you think and it is surprisingly easy to write that amount of words using the techniques you are about to learn. When you write a book this length, it is a good size in both electronic and printed format. When people receive the printed book they don't wonder why it is so thin and flimsy, they receive a good sized book, and their initial impressions are positive, which is very important.

You'll learn how to produce a book that people want to read, which is easier than you may think, and one that can continue to make you money for months, if not years to come!

If you feel you lack confidence in your skills as a writer, then you can easily improve them. Sites such as www.edx.org and www.coursera.org both offer high-quality writing courses for free! These courses are designed by some of the top universities in the world, and you can take them for absolutely nothing. These courses are great to learn more about the creative writing process, or about grammar and spelling and can help you become a better writer. For those that have an Apple device, there is iTunes University, which also has some great free writing courses.

It doesn't matter what your background is, if you apply yourself then you can turn writing into a full-time income. Best of all, once published books can continue to earn for years, allowing you to build up a solid income.

I must tell you that book sales are seasonal. In general, you see a big increase in book sales on the run up to Christmas and a slump around Easter and again around summer when people are away on vacation. Certain subjects sell well all year round, but others will only sell at certain times of the year. For example, gardening books tend to be popular in spring, when people are thinking about their garden. Self-help books are popular at the start of the year, as are diet books when people are full of New Year's Resolutions. Beauty books sell well just before summer when people want to look good while on their vacation.

The key is to understand this seasonality and to use it to your benefit. There are evergreen books, which sell all year consistently, and you will write some of those, but tapping into this seasonal market can give you a significant income boost several times a year. Personally, I love the run up to Christmas because my book sales go crazy. In a typical November I can see my book sales quadruple, which is a lovely bonus when Amazon pay out at the start of the New Year, sadly it doesn't arrive in time for Christmas.

There is a lot to learn, but I will walk you through all of it in this book and show you how you can become a published author yourself. The lovely thing about being self-published is you are in complete control of your books, and you can create a full-time income if you want. Some people are happy with just making a few hundred bucks more every month, whereas other people are pushing for the six or even seven figure income, both of which are entirely possible!

Enjoy learning to become a writer and publishing your book … it's an exciting, rewarding, and potentially life changing adventure.

SELF-PUBLISH, TRADITIONAL PUBLISHING OR HYBRID

There are three methods for you to publish your book and you need to understand all three before we move any further. Self-publishing is the approach I recommend, at least initially, but do not rule out the other two, they both have their uses and advantages.

The three methods are:

- Self-Publishing where you publish the book and do not use a publishing house
- Traditional Publishing which uses a publishing house
- Hybrid which is a combination of the above two

We are going to focus on self-publishing in this book but will mention the other methods as and when they are appropriate and necessary. Many authors will remain self-published, but some will approach traditional publishing houses too and become hybrid authors.

All of the above work, and it depends on your book and your personal circumstances as to which you will choose.

Self-Publishing

When you self-publish, you publish the book yourself, meaning you are responsible for all aspects of the publishing process from proof reading and editing to marketing. The upside of this is that you get all of the commission for selling your book, but you are entirely responsible for making those sales!

Most people will self-publish through Amazon, but you can self-publish through many other sites such as Kobo, Nook, Apple Books, Ingram Spark and more. To publish a book as a paperback you will need an ISBN. These are provided free by Amazon, or you can buy a block of ISBN numbers for your own use from Nielsen Books or Bowker. These are not cheap, which is why most people opt for publishing through Amazon where you are provided one for your paperback for free.

ISBN numbers uniquely identify a book and can only be used for one book. When you update the book, change the title or change the edition number, it will need a new ISBN. You can very quickly go through ISBN numbers, and it can get expensive, so think carefully about whether you need to invest in them or whether the numbers assigned by Amazon are suitable for your needs (they are all I use).

As a self-published author there are some major advantages:

- Keeping commissions – you keep 100% of all of the commissions that you make from sales
- Write what you want – there is no publisher to tell you what you can or cannot publish, you can write anything you want … which is both a good and a bad thing as you may not be as aware as a publisher of what is or is not selling
- Control over rights – you have complete control over your publishing rights and can do whatever you want with your books
- Control over artwork – you create the covers you want without a publisher trying to tell you what to do, but you are responsible for paying for it and have to find someone to create the cover for you
- Immediate publication – your book can be published as soon as you have finished it and can be available for sale within 24 to 72 hours. With traditional publishing, it can take a year or more for your book to actually hit the shelves, during which time you are living off any advance you may have received, which may not be as much as you hoped for
- Ease of updating – if you spot errors or just want to add more information, you can easily update your book and republish it with readers able to download the refreshed copy.
- Keeping your book relevant – as you can easily update your book, so you can add new information as and when it is available. This keeps your books relevant and stops them becoming dated, which can happen with traditional publishing

- Regular payments – CreateSpace pays you at the end of the month after the sale has been made, i.e. If you sell books in January, you will receive payment for them at the end of February. Kindle pays you sixty days after the end of the month the sales were made. This means that if you make sales in January, you won't see the payment until the end of March. Payments through traditional publishing can be quarterly, twice a year or even yearly!

There are also disadvantages to being self-published, including:

- Responsible for marketing – you are completely in charge of marketing your book and earning your commissions. If you are not good at marketing, then this can make it hard for you to earn decent money, but you will learn marketing techniques later in this book. There isn't anyone else to do it for you unless you hire someone
- Responsible for editing and proof reading – you either have to proof read and edit your book yourself, persuade a friend to do it for free or hire a professional to do it for you, which isn't cheap
- Bearing all costs – any costs relating to publishing your book are all your responsibility, including cover design, marketing, proof copies of your books and more
- Lack of knowledge of publishing industry – you may not have a good knowledge of the publishing industry and could find some aspects of self-publishing difficult, though we'll cover those as you go through the rest of this book. You may also be less aware of trends in the industry and what is and is not, popular

Self-publishing is by far the easiest way to get your books to market and to start earning. As a self-published author, you get regularly paid by the sites you are published on, whereas with traditional publishing you can get paid as infrequently as once a year! My personal recommendation is that you start off with self-publishing. It is quicker, easier and gets you results rapidly. Once you have written some books and had some experience, then you can approach a traditional publishing house and become a hybrid author.

Traditional Publishing

Most people are familiar with traditional publishing, and the majority of books you see in book stores come from the traditional publishing houses.

This approach is long-winded and slow, involving you sending a query letter to a publisher, detailing what you are proposing to write. After weeks, but usually months, they will respond to your query. If they respond positively, then you start to write the book. If they do not, then you move on to the next publisher. Some publishers require exclusive queries, meaning you cannot send the query to any other publisher until they have responded, but others do not require this.

Once you have signed the contract, you need to write the book and have it completed by the agreed deadline. Usually, around this time, you will get an advance, which could be anything from a few hundred dollars up, depending on how well the publisher feels your book will do. Once the publisher has recouped this advance, then you will be paid royalties on the books you sell.

Although the process is slow, and it can take years for your book actually to be on sale, many people at least like to try this approach. There is a feeling amongst some people that unless you have been traditionally published, you are not a 'real' author. However, whichever route to publishing you take, you are still a real author and these days, more and more people are moving to self-publishing because of the flexibility and control.

However, traditional publishing has some advantages and is still a very viable solution for some authors.

- Access to expert advice – publishing houses are full of experts, and you will have access to them for everything from story development, title creation, cover creation and more. This can be really helpful for you as they will know what works and what doesn't work in your genre. However, it can be frustrating when you want to take a particular approach to your book, and the publisher doesn't like it
- Fewer out of pocket expenses – the publisher is responsible for meeting all the costs of marketing and producing your book. This is recouped from sales of your book. This means you don't have to spend any money on creating a cover, hiring an editor and so on
- Professional proof reading and editing – as part of the publishing process, your book will be proof read and edited by professionals. Your book will be improved, grammar, punctuation, spelling and sentence structure will be analyzed and corrected. The upside of this is that it is very expensive to hire someone to do this for you, but the downside is it can be a slow process, further delaying publication of your book
- Potential global marketing – your publishing house will be able to distribute your book globally to book shops, Amazon and all the other online book retailers. This gives you access to large markets, but they could easily decide to only distribute in certain territories,

and there is nothing you can do to get wider distribution
- Potentially large advance – the size of the advance is a direct indication of how successful the publishing company thinks your book will be. A large advance means they think your book will sell extremely well, whereas an advance of a few thousand dollars means they do not think your book will sell particularly well. The downside of this is that this advance is taken out of your royalties, i.e. You don't get any royalties until the advance has been paid back

But it also has some disadvantages.

- Tends towards more popular books – traditional publishers will only publish books that they think will sell well. Therefore, they will usually only accept mainstream books that they can see have potential. However, this does mean they are very blinkered and often pass over books that could be huge successes. The Harry Potter books, which have become a global phenomenon were turned down by a number of publishers who thought they were dreadful!
- Very slow to get your book on the shelf – from first contacting a publishing to your book appearing on bookshelves can take a year or more. The process is unbelievably slow when you consider I can write a 20,000-word book in a week and have it published and made its first sale on Sunday night! This lack of speed comes down to the processes of developmental editing, proof reading and so on. For some authors, this tortoise like approach is too much, particularly if you can produce books relatively quickly
- Difficult to update books - it is almost impossible to update books that are traditionally published. Unless there is a significant rewrite, the publishers will not go to the effort of making any changes. The upside of self-publishing is that if there are new developments in the field my book is in, I can update my book with the new information, and it is available in less than 72 hours to readers. This can do a lot for sales because your book is always up to date and has the latest information in. Often with traditional publishing, your book is out of date before it has hit the shelves, which makes this not suitable for books in fields which change frequently, e.g. Internet or technology
- Royalty payments less frequent – traditional publishers pay royalties every quarter, every six months or, in some cases, every year. This can make it very hard for you to manage your cash flow when you think that Amazon pays monthly on CreateSpace sales and 60 days after the month of the sale with Kindle sales. It will depend on the

publisher and your contract as to how and when you get paid

- Lack of control over publishing process – you have no control over the publishing process and will be guided (think strong-armed) through much of it. Although it is your book, the publishing house will guide you to what they feel is best and will make the book successful, rather than what you want to do with your book. Although their advice can sometimes be good, some authors dislike the lack of ability to express themselves artistically
- Publishing obligation – your contract may state that you have to do book tours, appear on television or other promotional activities for your book. You are contractually obliged to fulfill these tasks which you may or may not want to or may be inconvenient.

Traditional publishing was, for a long time, the only way to get a book published. With the rise of Amazon and other online book retailers, you now may self-publish without spending any money. Although a lot of authors aspire to traditional publishing, they prefer the flexibility and speed of self-publishing.

Hybrid Publishing

Hybrid publishing is very simply where an author is both self-published and traditionally published. This is an approach some authors are taking these days and which some publishing houses are more than happy to follow.

People are taking this approach for one of two reasons. Firstly, they have been self-published and then approach traditional publishers with new books having a track record of success and a fan base, which makes the book more likely to be a success. Secondly, authors will take this approach if they are publishing books wildly different from their usual genre, i.e. They are traditionally published and want to branch out into a completely different subject area so self-publish either under their name or a pen name.

This has a lot of advantages and combines the benefits of both worlds. It will allow you to publish your own books while your more mainstream books benefit from a traditional publisher.

The Dangers of Vanity Presses

Vanity presses are one of the snares that trap many aspiring authors, so it is very important that I warn you of this approach and explain what it is.

There are some publishing houses out there that appear to be traditional publishers. Although they will take any book they see has a chance of commercial success, they will usually insist on payments from you to publish your book.

If any publisher insists that you pay to publish your book, run away. Seriously. You are going to end up paying several thousand dollars and maybe get a few printed copies of your book. You will not get the support and marketing muscle needed to sell your book, which means you are unlikely to ever see any royalty payments.

These publishing houses are very insistent and will be in almost constant contact with you trying to persuade you to publish with them, but you should avoid them. They rely on gullible new authors who want to be published, and you will end up paying several thousand dollars for a few copies of your book and no rights to do anything with it.

Before approaching any publisher, search online for their name and the word 'review.' You will be able to find information about the publisher from other authors and will be able to find out whether or not they are genuine. Far too many authors fall into their traps and find their book is published, making no sales, and there is nothing they can do about it for several years until rights to the book return to you.

These companies look very attractive and are very persuasive, but always search online for reviews to check they are a genuine publisher. They will make you all sorts of offers and will accept almost any book, which makes you feel great that a traditional publisher is interested in you, but afterward you realize the book isn't marketed and no royalties are forthcoming.

Grammar, Spelling, & Punctuation

This is the part where many potential authors groan or decide they really can't be an author. Before you do, these are all something you can learn, have done for you, or use software to correct!

Grammar, spelling, and punctuation are absolutely vital to any published book. Readers are slightly more forgiving in eBooks, but in printed books they are much less tolerant. If you look on Amazon for reviews of self-published books, this is the number one complaint from readers.

The problem with errors here is that they jerk the reader out of their state of enjoyment of a book. In fiction, it can pull them out of the world you have created, making it hard for them to get absorbed in your story. In nonfiction, it is just annoying and can seriously mess up your message, e.g. Writing 'cool' instead of 'cook.' In children's books, it is just a big no-no as parents want their children to read the right spelling of words.

If you struggle with these, then you can take online classes or classes at a local college to help you improve your skills. It is worth doing this as words are your craft, and you need to be able to write well to sell lots of books and make good money.

You can proof read your books yourself, but you will find that as you have written the book, you will not catch all the errors yourself. If your budget is tight, then get a friend or family member to proof read your books.

If you have the budget, then you can hire a professional to do the job. Depending on what you need doing and how long your book is, this can run into the hundreds of dollars. Developmental editing, where the editor reads your story, ensures it is consistent and helps make the story better, is more expensive than plain proofreading where they just check for errors.

This is a vital part of producing a book and is not something you should avoid. Selling books is a competitive market, and if you are getting poor reviews online because your book has easily correctable errors in, then you are going to struggle to make sales.

When I started out I didn't proof read properly, I will admit that I didn't know what I was doing and thought I could write well. Once the reviews of the first couple of books came in, and I saw they were criticizing the books for typos I realized the importance of it. Unfortunately, the books already had negative reviews, but I republished the corrected book and responded to the reviews, stating that the book had been updated and fortunately, they sold well. However, I could have avoided the poor reviews by making sure the book was edited properly in the first place.

For people who do not speak English as the first language, editing is even more important. Many other languages construct sentences differently to how they would in the English language which appears awkward to native speakers. Unfortunately, to many native speakers, this will be seen as a negative and can generate poor reviews, harming the sale of your book.

If English is not your native language, then you must get a native speaker to review your book and provide editorial advice. The same goes for anyone who is writing in any language other than their native tongue. Get it proof read by a native speaker to ensure that the language is correct.

One of the main problems people have, even native speakers, is the difference in spelling in the English language between the US and the United Kingdom and the difference in what words mean in the two countries. This is a hotly debated subject and one in which you will have to decide where you stand.

The Different Types of English

There is UK (British) English, Australian English, Canadian English and American English. All of which, although the same language, have fundamental differences. For example, UK English ends some words in -ise, e.g. Compromise, whereas in US English, these words end in -ize, e.g. Compromize. Americans also drop the U from the UK English words colour (color), armour (armor), favourite (favorite), neighbour (neighbor) and so on.

There are also a lot of differences in meanings in words too between UK and US English. Gas in American is Petrol in English. Trunk is boot, faucet is tap, rutabaga is turnip and so on.

To make it even more complex, there are differences in sentence construction and the use of certain words. British people use the words 'actually' and 'whilst', but these are virtually absent from American English.

This can make it very difficult for non-Americans to write books for the American market. In some cases, and this has happened to me, I have had negative reviews left on my books because I have used UK English (I am from the UK) in my books.

This is a contentious subject, with many non-American authors militantly declaring they will not write in American. However, we have to be realistic. The American market is by far the largest market for books in the world. Approximately 80-85% of my sales every single month come from America. Less than 10% of my sales are from the United Kingdom with the rest being from other countries.

Let's think about this for a second. Are you going to write your book in a way which is potentially off-putting to 80-85% of your target market?

Of course, you are not. In the majority of cases, you will need to learn to write in American English. Unless you are writing a fiction book that is based in England, or you are specifically writing for an English, Canadian or Australian market, you need to write in American English. Set the language in your word processor to US English and correct any errors that you find. Get your book proof read by an American to make sure that all the language does well.

Some books will work without being written in American English, but, particularly when starting out, you need to write to your target market.

I know this is a subject that people feel very strongly about, but my argument has always been I am writing to my target market. Certain books I will write two versions, one for the USA market, and one for the UK market. For example, if I was writing a book on rutabaga recipes, it wouldn't sell in the UK because nobody knows what a rutabaga is, but Americans do, and it would sell well. For the UK market, I would have to do a find and replace in the document, changing the word rutabaga to turnip, which will be understood in the UK market.

You have to decide what is best for you, and that depends on the subject of your book. Most non-Americans are comfortable reading US English, but most Americans are not comfortable reading non-US English.

Benefiting From Spell Checkers

Most word processors come with grammar and spell checkers these days. I use Microsoft Word to write in with an Office 365 subscription, which means I pay monthly to use it. I can spell check in both UK and US English, plus it has a grammar checker.

I strongly recommend using these before you send your book off to an editor as it will save a lot of time. The software will find and correct a lot of errors, but there are some it will miss.

You can use an online service such as Grammarly, which many authors swear by. This is a good resource if you are on a limited budget and will help to correct your book and reduce the risk of any complaints about poor spelling. With Grammarly, sign up to their mailing list before you buy, and they will send you special offers. After a few weeks, you will receive discount offers from them for as much as 40%, making it worth your while waiting until you receive a discount to sign up.

It is important that you use software tools if you are not going to hire an editor. It will save a lot of time and highlight any issues with your book.

My personal approach is to write my book, and then I will run the spell check in Microsoft Word, correcting any errors. Then I will go through my nonfiction books and add pictures to the book (top tip if using pictures – you can compress them within Word which reduces your file size and delivery charges from Amazon). As I am adding pictures, I am proof reading the book, changing content and adding more information (like this) when I feel it needs it.

I will catch 80-90% of errors with this method, but I still hand it to someone else to proof read to catch those mistakes I don't find. Fortunately for me, my wife is very good at proof reading and does mine for me. Otherwise I would have to hire someone. We'll talk more about hiring people for these jobs later on in this book.

It is very important for your book to be well received and perceived as professional to have the spelling, grammar, and punctuation correct. The biggest complaint about Indie, or self-published, books is that they are poorly edited. If you take the time to get these right, then your book will instantly stand out from the multitude of other books vying for readers attention. You are more likely to get positive reviews, which means an increase in sales.

SETTING UP YOUR WRITING BUSINESS

Now you know how profitable and easy writing can be, you will be keen to set yourself up in business as a writer. This isn't particularly hard to do and you will may already have some of what you need at home.

This chapter is all about how to set up your writing business and what you will need to write. You will learn the tools of the trade that you need as well as how to balance your working time with your day job and home life.

Registering Your Business

The first thing you need to do is set yourself up correctly as a business. This is going to vary significantly from country to country and even from state to state. This is vital because you can get in serious trouble if you do not.

This means you need to register yourself as a business, if required, and inform the necessary officials that you are a business, i.e. Registering to pay tax on your earnings as an author.

I am going to stress now that this is absolutely essential and you have to do this. You may think that you can get away with not paying tax on your earnings. You may be able to for a year or two, but they will catch up with you, and when they do you will realize they make the mafia look like fun people to invite around for tea! Amazon gathers tax details from you when you sign up, and this is reported to local tax authorities.

Legally registering your business means you can work to build a business knowing that you aren't hiding from the taxman or other legal authority. It means your earnings are yours to keep after you have paid the appropriate taxes and you have nothing to worry about.

I would recommend that you employ an accountant because a lot of the expenses you are going to occur as an author can be offset against your tax. For example, equipment you buy such as a laptop, your book covers, costs of editors and so on, can all be off-set against your earnings to reduce the amount of tax you pay. If you are not able to employ an accountant on a monthly basis, then at least hire one at the end of the year to go over your accounts. Engage them for a couple of hours when starting your business so they can advise you on what you can and cannot claim as a business expense.

This is worth a lot of money to you as a good accountant could save you thousands of dollars, or more, every year.

Equipment

Starting a business as a writer is probably one of the cheapest businesses out there! The costs are minimal. All you really need to start writing is:

1. A word processor – this can be on a laptop, desktop, Apple Mac or tablet. It is entirely up to you what you write on. You will need some software to write with, which could be Microsoft Word, Open Office, Vellum or anything else that allows you to write and format a document. It depends on what you are familiar with.
2. An Internet connection – you require this to research and publish your books.

Although this is all you need to get started, other items are useful to you.

- Stock Photograph Subscription – this is important for nonfiction because it allows you to put good quality, relevant pictures in your books. Although you can find royalty free pictures online, it can be hard finding something that is relevant. You'll learn more about pictures later on in this book.
- Adobe Photoshop – for anyone planning on doing their own book covers, this is the best photo editor on the market. GIMP (careful searching online for this) is a free alternative that a lot of people use.
- Grammarly Subscription - very useful to check your grammar if you are not going to hire a proof reader or editor.
- Office 365 Subscription – for an affordable monthly payment you get access to all of the Microsoft office programs, including Microsoft Word. It also gives you 15GB of OneDrive storage, which is rather handy!

- Vellum (Mac only) – this only works on iMac's but is considered the Rolls Royce of book formatting software and is well worth the investment to create beautiful looking books. This isn't for everyone as you need an iMac, which has a significant price tag on it.

Pretty much, that is all you need. Personally, I also have a stills camera and video camera. I take a lot of pictures that I use in my books, which helps me avoid copyright issues and ensures I have relevant pictures, which does help sales. I also record videos which I upload to my YouTube channels to help promote my books.

Backing Up Your Work

This is one of the most important things you can do to keep your writing safe. The last thing you want is to lose 50,000 words of your book (trust me, that is not fun).

How you back up your work is your decision depending on what is available to you.

Firstly, do not keep the only copy of your books on a USB key or other portable drive. Lose the drive, and you lose your books. USB keys have a habit of going wrong, and you can plug it into your computer to find it suddenly blank with no data on.

Likewise, do not keep the only copy of your books on a computer or tablet. If something goes wrong with it, then you lose all of your work.

I spent many years working as an IT professional before I became an author, so can advise you on good solutions for this.

My recommendation is that your books are stored in three locations:

1. Locally on a hard drive of the computer, you are working on
2. On a removable device, e.g. USB stick
3. In the cloud

There are lots of different ways of doing this. I store all my files in OneDrive, which I have as part of my Office 365 subscription. This is synchronized with both my desktop and laptop, so the files are automatically backed up to those devices every time I log in. All my writing is done on an iPad Pro with a Bluetooth keyboard, accessing the files on the OneDrive. Once a week, all the files are copied to a USB key which is carefully hidden away in the back of a desk drawer.

This solution works well for me and allows me access to my files pretty much anywhere. It gives me security as I know, no matter what, my files are safe. If my laptop dies, my files are on OneDrive. If my desktop dies, my files are on OneDrive, if my iPad gets lost or stolen, my files are on OneDrive. If OneDrive blows up overnight then at most, I will lose a couple of days work, but the files are synced on my laptop and desktop.

You can store your files in the iCloud, Google Drive, or anywhere else you want, but at the very least, your files need to be in some sort of cloud storage. Your files are your business and I cannot emphasise strongly enough how important it is that you keep these files safe. Losing them can cost you a lot of money and have a major impact on your business. Think carefully about how to keep your business safe; it will pay off.

Working Time

Finding the time to write can be difficult if you have to juggle a family with a day job. The more you write, the more you can publish and the more you can earn. Writing a thousand words a week will mean it can take months before you publish your book, so you need to find time to get your writing done.

Set aside time when you will not be disturbed so that you can concentrate on your writing. Some people can write while watching television with the family (which I am now), but other people cannot do this.

Depending on your schedule you will have to work out when you can write. Get up an hour earlier in the morning and spend that time writing. Write during your lunch break at work, write when the kids are having a nap or are at school. Write in the evening, even if it just for an hour.

The more you can write, the more you can publish and the quicker you will achieve your income goals. There will be limitations on the time you can spend writing, but try to organize your life to give you the time you need. This is easier if you have the support of your friends and family as they can help you, but find ways to get the time you need to build your business.

Working Space

You will need somewhere to work as an author, which can be hard for some people to find as they lack space in their home.

If you have a spare room to set up as an office or a room where you can put a desk in the corner, then that is fantastic. For many people, their working space is perched on the sofa with a laptop on their knee.

Arrange your home so that you have somewhere to write and focus on being a successful author. Alternatively, head to a local café where you can sit and write while enjoying a nice coffee, which is not an allowable business expense by the way!

Although renting an office to run your business from may sound wonderful, it is an expense you may not be able to bear initially. Once your publishing business starts making enough money to cover the cost, then you could look into it if you cannot work from home or you want to differentiate between working time and home time.

Managing Your Money

This is an important subject to talk about, though some people will have more money to invest in their writing business than others. I started with $0 to invest, whereas other writers I know have spent thousands on their books.

I would recommend working out how much you can afford to spend on your business each month. Then you need to stick to this budget, open a separate bank account for your business and pay all expenses out of this. Every month, transfer the money you are investing into this account, and if you cannot afford to pay for something for your business, you don't buy it until you have the money in this account. This allows you to keep tight control over your expenses and ensure that you do not spend more money than you can afford or get into debt starting your business.

It is best if you keep a tight control on your business expenses because it is very easy for you to overspend and find yourself having spent more money than you have earned. The biggest mistake I see authors make is to throw money at their business without worrying about their return on investment, particularly when it comes to advertising and promotions.

Spending money to grow your business is a great idea, and every business does this. The problem comes when you are spending money without knowing whether or not it has made you any sales and increased your income.

For example, you book five promotional events on one day and make one hundred sales of your book. How many sales did each promotional event make?

You have no idea and no way of knowing. For all you know, one promo made a hundred sales and the others didn't make any sales at all.

You can see why it is important to track your spend, particularly on advertising, and tie it in with sales. If you run a promo and it makes a lot of sales then you can either run it again for the same book to try and make more sales or run it for the next book on a similar subject. If you run a promo and it doesn't make any sales, you know not to run it again because it doesn't give you any return on your investment.

It is very important you think carefully before spending money on your business. Decide what you need to buy, look around for the best prices and then determine how much of an impact it will have on your profitability.

There is nothing wrong with going out and spending $5000 on advertising if it is going to make you $20,000 in sales, but if you are spending that amount of money and making $100 in sales, then you've got a serious problem. Likewise, spending $1000 on a book cover is a great idea if it is going to bring in thousands of sales, but if you are spending that amount on a book cover, making a trickle of sales and getting negative reviews, then you are wasting your time and money.

The two most important aspects of running your business are to keep control of your finances and know your figures. You need to know that your business can support any expenditure and that whatever you are spending is going to earn your investment back.

I would recommend at the very least, taking a short bookkeeping course so that you can learn how to track your income and expenditure correctly. This will save you a lot of time when filing your taxes and ensure you keep track of your finances.

When you are tracking your income and expenditure, you will know exactly how much money you have available, whether you can afford to buy book covers, advertising or promos and so on. Without a good knowledge of your figures, you will be driving your business further and further into the red until the amount of expenditure becomes unsustainable. It is at this point most people quit and tell everyone that being an author doesn't work.

It does work, but like any business, if you are spending more than you are earning, your business will collapse. For years, Amazon was spending hundreds of millions of dollars a year, yet making back a fraction of what they were earning. In their first couple of years, most experts didn't believe

Amazon would make it, but they persisted, expanded their business aggressively and became a household name.

But they are the exception rather than the rule. I have seen people start their own business, spend money like water and then fold their business, deeply in debt because they haven't managed to make the income to match the expenditure. It is no good you constantly spending money thinking that the exposure will do you good. If people aren't buying your books, then you may as well burn the money to keep warm in winter as no amount of promos are going to work!

When you are an author, you can research your books before you start writing and spend any money. By identifying the correct genres and niches, you can almost guarantee you will make money. Once you have identified the area to write in, your next step is to create a killer book that will fly off the shelves. All of this will be discussed as you progress through this book.

Just remember, keep a close eye on your business finances, don't spend more than you can afford, and make sure you know your return on investment for any expenditure.

Creating A Business Plan

This is one aspect of starting a business that 99% of authors will completely ignore, but I feel is probably one of the most important steps you can take.

A business plan outlines what you are going to do as a business, how you will operate your business and how much money it will make. If you are serious about creating a profitable business, this is vital because it helps you plan what you are going to do. Your business plan can also be used to approach banks for business loans and to help keep you motivated when you are struggling.

There are plenty of templates online for writing a business plan, and which you use will depend on where in the world you live. Different countries have different requirements for the layout and format, but essentially they all have similar content.

Typically, a business plan is written detailing your actions over the next year in detail but also containing projections and outlines for the next five or even ten years.

Your business plan needs to contain the following information, as a minimum:

- Outline of business – what you are proposing to do as a business, e.g. Writing books, but with more detail about genres/niches
- Publishing schedule – details of how often you are going to publish books, just make sure this is realistic

- Writing plan – describes the books you are going to write and when you are going to write them, e.g. Teaching Your Cat To Dance written by March, Teaching Your Dog To Sing written by April, Teaching Your Hamster to Somersault written by June. This helps to keep you focused and stops you getting distracted with new ideas, ending up with a hard drive full of partially finished books. This schedule should be flexible, but you need to be disciplined and finish the books you've started unless you have a very good reason not to

- Earnings projections – this is harder to do unless you have published some books and know what sort of earnings you can expect. However, you can estimate from looking at the categories you are going to publish in and also base it on your income requirements. Remember that you do not get 100% of your sale price, but a percentage, which will be discussed in detail later

- Expenditure – detail what monthly expenses you will have such as your book covers, editing, website costs, mailing lists costs and so on. Also, detail your capital expenditures, e.g. Buying a laptop or computer and so on so you know what you need to buy and the costs. How you deal with these costs will depend upon your tax laws

- Business structure – define how you are going to set up your business. Will it be an LLC? Will you operate as a sole trader? It depends on your individual circumstances, but it must be thought about right at the start, so you are operating legally

- Business location – where are you going to run your business? Does your mortgage or rental agreement allow you to run a business from home? Do you need to rent an office? Again, this is very individual and will reflect your personal circumstances

- Permits and insurances – detail any permits you need to run your business as well as any insurances required. These will vary from country to country and state to state

- Market research – look at the niches you want to publish in and determine what type of books are selling, who the top authors are, and what these top authors are doing right, e.g. Cover styles, blurb, book titles and so on

- Seasonality – analyze your market and determine if there is any seasonality in sales in your proposed niches. You don't want to see your income plummet unexpectedly because nobody is buying your books that month. Outline what you can do to combat this fluctuation in sales and even out your income

There is a lot more you can include in your business plan, but this is the essential information to keep you focused and working to a plan rather than being all over the place. Take the time to work on this because it can not only to help you clarify what you are doing but can be used to convince the people around you that you are not wasting your time being an author.

When I decided to take writing seriously, I spent almost two months writing my business plan, researching my niches and detailing a year's worth of writing. Once I had completed the earnings projections, I was stunned by how much I could be earning in a year if I stuck to my plan. It was extremely motivating, and every time I felt myself losing focus, I referred to the plan to get myself back on track.

I also used my business plan to get a business loan to fund buying the equipment I needed to make writing easier for me. This was approved very quickly because I had a solid plan. I also showed it to my wife to get family support with moving the business forward, and the information gained me the support to focus on the business and take it seriously.

This is something a lot of people miss out because it requires some work. It doesn't have to take you two months like it took me, but can be done in a few hours. I strongly recommend you complete a business plan because it will help you a lot on the dark days, and you will have those, to keep you focused and remind you what you are working towards.

COMPONENTS OF A COMPELLING BOOK

So what does make a compelling book?

This is the secret that authors across the world are desperate to know and over the next few chapters we will analyze successful books and determine exactly what a book needs to make sales and be successful.

Firstly, though, what is a successful book?

This is very subjective and will depend on the author. For Stephen King, a successful book is a New York Times bestseller, shipping several million copies. For a first time author though, a successful book may sell half a dozen books in its first week.

It's important that you define what a successful book is for you, This will depend on your genre or niche, your experience, the promos you have booked and more. You will need to look at the niche you are releasing your book in to see how many copies a book could sell.

The categories you have listed your book in will also influence the number of sales you make. Some categories are more competitive and more popular than others, with the bestselling books selling hundreds or thousands of copies every day. Other categories are like a ghost town, with few, if any sales each day.

Here are some of the key components that a compelling book has, listed in no particular order, and all will be talked about as you continue to go through this book.

- Good quality content – the content of your book needs to be good quality both in content and in the layout
- Well written content – your content needs to be well written, with good grammar, good sentence construction, good spelling and so on
- An interesting and engaging style of writing – writing in a dry, boring style is going to put people off reading your book, making it hard work. Write in an engaging and interesting style that is appropriate for your audience. For example, if you are writing a book about law then your style of writing will be professional and a little dry. However, if you are writing about gardening, then your book will be written in a less formal, more light-hearted style
- An eye catching book cover – the cover really does sell your books, and if your cover does not grab attention then you still struggle to get people to look at your book
- An attention grabbing title – a title should be punchy and to the point. A long winded title is going to put people off. If necessary, use a short, punchy title and then use a sub-title to go into more detail
- Interesting blurb – when people look at your book online they will read the blurb or description of your book. If this is poorly written, boring or full of mistakes, then you won't make sales. It needs to be engaging, tell people what they are going to get, without giving away too much, and leave them wanting more, i.e. To buy the book
- Relevant and useful information in the book (nonfiction) – the content of the book needs to be relevant, useful and up to date. Poorly researched or information that is wrong is going to get you refunds, negative reviews and stop you building a profitable business
- An engaging storyline that the reader can immerse themselves in (fiction) – think about the fiction books you have enjoyed and spent money on yourself. Were they interesting or boring? What did you do with the last boring book you read? I remember clearly the last boring book I read, it was dreadfully written, poorly formatted and the story was just tedious. I stopped after half a dozen pages. You must grab your reader's attention with the first page and leave them wanting to read more.

As you continue to read through this book, you will learn more about the components of a successful book and how you can avoid the mistakes most new authors make. This is going to help you start earning quicker, and hopefully help you avoid creating a dud book.

The key to creating a compelling book is to have an in-depth understanding of your readers and what they want. Do your research properly, and you will know exactly what content people are looking for and can create a book that will sell well.

Choosing a Nonfiction Niche

This can be a stumbling block for someone starting out as an author. What do you write about?

Some people will advise that you write about something you know, but what if there is no market for that? If you can do this and it makes money, then that is great, but otherwise, you need to write for the market where the money is. Don't worry if you aren't an expert on the subject, you will learn later on how to quickly and easily become an expert on pretty much anything!

For some people, their hobbies will be profitable niches, but for other people, their hobbies will literally be vanity books; books that are published for fun and enjoyment rather than to make money. There is nothing wrong with this sort of publishing, but I'm sure you would prefer to publish books that are going to make you money.

How to Research A Niche

Although you can write a book on any subject, to make money, you need to choose a subject, or niche, which people are spending money in. Unsurprisingly, this is where most people struggle because there are so many different subjects you could write about and it can be difficult to determine which is the best for you.

Firstly, you need to look through the Amazon bestsellers list, which can be found at www.amazon.com/bestsellers. This is a list of the top 100 selling products in every category on Amazon, from bicycles to books to pet food. It's a great tool for researching what is selling and what is not.

There are two potential areas you are interested in, the books category and the Kindle category. I'd suggest the latter as it contains more books, particularly self-published books, and you are most interested in competing with those rather than traditionally published books from the big publishing houses.

Drill down through the different categories under the Kindle Store and Kindle Ebooks section and look at different areas. As we are concentrating on nonfiction, avoid any of the fiction categories, though this process is the same if you are looking at profitable fiction niches.

Look at the top 100 for a variety of different sections. As we are firstly picking topics, you aren't interested in much more than the subject of the book.

Let's look at the self-help section, and remember this will have changed by the time you read this, but the principles are the important part. This is a subject area many Indie authors tackle because it is a multi-billion dollar market and books sell quite well, even when written by new authors.

Firstly, anything written by a celebrity can be discounted during this research because their status skews sales and it may be their status is what is making the book sell, but for anyone else, sales would be difficult.

When I search this category, in the top one hundred, there are several books on mindfulness, several on decluttering your mind, several on improving your memory and some on how habits can help you improve your life.

As there is more than one book on the subject in the top 100, it means that it is a subject that sells well, particularly as most of these books are not by a celebrity or well-known authors. That means all of these are potentially good subjects to write about.

As you are doing this research, pay attention to both the covers, titles, and descriptions of the best-selling books. These are all going to come in useful later on in this process.

Then start to look at the titles you've identified. A pen and paper can be used here to write down relevant information.

Take a note of how long each book is and how many stars it has. You are looking for details of how many pages the book is and will look at the lengths of some books to find out how long your book needs to be to meet market expectations.

Then look at the Amazon Best Sellers Rank. If this is below 20,000, then the book is selling very well. The lower this rank, the better the book is selling. If all of the books you've identified on a subject have a good sales rank, then it means it is potentially a very profitable niche. You may need to do some advertising as it could be highly competitive, but the money is there, so it is worth exploring.

Go through the best sellers list and identify six to ten different subjects, not all in the self-help niche, that you could write about. Remember, you are looking for multiple books in the top 100 best sellers on the subject and books that have a good sales rank. Write these subjects down as you will look into them more later.

Boosting Your Income Further
As you are looking at these books, you are looking for books that are evergreen, i.e. Books that will sell consistently year in and year out. Parenthood, for example, is a subject that is never going to go out of fashion, people will always buy books on the subject. Something like the 2020 Olympics may hit the bestseller list during the event but will soon fade into obscurity.

The subjects you identify need to be ones where there is continuous demand. It doesn't matter if it is seasonal, such as people only want the information at Christmas or during the summer. It does matter if the information will fade into obscurity and be irrelevant in a few weeks or months.

You are looking for subjects that will sell both as a physical book and as an e-book. Printed books are extremely profitable, particularly in the nonfiction niches, so you need to make sure your book works in both formats.

Some niches, such as recipe books, don't tend to work well as Indie published physical books because they do not contain enough pictures. For recipe books, people want glossy, full-color books which you will struggle to produce economically, but for many other books, they sell very well. However, people do buy recipe books just in the Kindle version. A physical book needs to be at least 15,000 words in length for it to feel substantial enough to be printed. Anything shorter than this and it looks more like a pamphlet than a book and people may question its value for money, which can lead to negative reviews.

There is a third potential stream of income for your books too. You can convert them into audio books which are distributed via a number of platforms including Audible. Not all subjects convert to audio books, recipe books are one that does not, but many others will work as an audio book. Check on Audible for the subjects you are considering and see how the audio versions are selling. Most people do not convert their books into audio format, and it can be done at no cost to yourself, which you will find out later in this book.

Writing a Series and Sequels
In an ideal world, your nonfiction book will either become a series, or it will lend itself to a sequel or two. Once people have bought one book from you, they are much more likely to buy another, providing they enjoyed the first book. Assuming they have, you have a great opportunity to market your other books on the same or similar subjects to them.

You will get some read through, where people start off with one of your books and buy more. In many nonfiction subjects, you tend to buy more than one book by authors you like. Alternatively, if you don't buy another of their books fairly soon, you will buy a book by them again when you need additional information.

This can work in your favor and help you make more sales, so while you are researching niches, look for one that can become a series or at least multiple books on the subject. If the first book sells well, then you can write other books on the subject.

Having multiple books on a single topic can establish you as an expert or authority on your chosen subject. Being considered an expert by your target market will help you make sales. Each of your books can also appear on the bestseller lists, which can also help you make more sales as people think you are an expert on the subject.

I have several books published in one particular niche and sales were slow, to be honest with you. Then one of my books got into a top 100 list, then another until I had about four or five books at any one time on ten to twelve different best seller lists. There is a noticeable increase in sales when the books are on these lists and the higher up the list the book climbs, the more it sells. It appears that Amazon favors books which are in the bestseller lists in some way. Buyers seem to use these lists to help them find books, so you really need to get your books into these best seller lists.

How do you do that?

Firstly, a good quality book. Secondly, get reviews and thirdly, promotion. All of these will be covered in more detail as you continue to read this book.

Making More Money From Your Book

Although your book sales are going to make you some money, you wouldn't turn down the opportunity to make extra money, would you?

Creating a series of books in a single niche means that you can build a list of email addresses and market to them. Build yourself a following on social media and market new releases to them, though be sure to have one account per niche, so you don't upset or confuse your readers.

All of these mean you have a list of people who are interested in your subject and willing to spend money. By building your social media presence, you will have a group of people you can instantly advertise your book to when it is released and make sales.

Also, work on building an email list from your books and market to your readers through email. The advantage of this is that you can not only sell your own books but also sell other people's books and products as an affiliate and earn extra money! We will discuss this further later on, but by giving away a free book or free information, you can encourage people to give you their email address which you can then earn money from by sending them emails!

As a final way to boost your money, think about how you can turn your book into a multimedia course or a membership site or even a face to face course. All of these are ways by which you can increase your profits, and trust me when I say this can easily dwarf the earnings from your book!

Your book may retail at $2.99 in Kindle form and say $9.99 in paperback. But what if your book showed people the value of your information and then directed them to a page where they could buy a course from you for $47? This course gave them valuable information and led them into another, more in depth course which costs $197. From this, they are funneled into your live seminars at $497 or $997 or into your personal coaching program at $1997 or $3997?

Can you see the potential here?

This is something that you must think about while you are writing your book and picking your niches as it is potentially a game changer. By converting your book into a course or training program, you can easily see a massive jump in your income.

These are additional considerations to make when you are picking your genre. It should not make you avoid a niche as many profitable niches will not translate into these types of products or courses, but there are many that will, and if you choose a niche that does, you can significantly boost your income.

FICTION VS. NONFICTION

This is another hotly debated subject and which you will write will depend on you. Some people want to write fiction; other people do not. There are pros and cons about both, and it depends on whether you are writing purely to make money or following your passion as to which you choose. Some people find fiction difficult; some people find nonfiction difficult. In my opinion, fiction is much harder as you have to produce a very good book to make money, but the opportunities to hit the big time are significant.

Fiction has a lot of benefits including:

- Wide variety of different genres you can write in
- Can hit the big time with just a few books
- Mostly sells e-books, volume of physical books sold is extremely low
- Sales through expanded distribution also tends to be low
- Usually, benefits from being in the KDP Select program as they can get a lot of page reads
- High read through rates through a series of good quality books
- Many books have key features (tropes) which feature in all good quality books, e.g. Dystopian future often features a strong female lead, this reduces the need for unique story ideas as people expect these patterns to be followed in all books in a genre (think about the Twilight series of books and all of its copy-cats or The Hunger Games)

In fiction, the sheer volume of genres means you can be very flexible and either write to what the market wants or write what you are passionate about.

Popular genres include romance (of any type), young adult, paranormal romance, erotica, fantasy, monster erotica, dystopian future and sci-fi with its various sub-genres.

Fiction benefits from setting up pre-orders, more so than nonfiction, as people will buy book one in your series and then pre-order other books if they enjoyed the story and others are not available. Just be warned, if you set up a pre-order, do not miss the deadline as Amazon will ban you for a year from setting up other pre-orders. Pre-orders are a great way to make money on books you haven't published yet from readers who enjoyed your book and must be used. It means you can promote books that are not finished and benefit further from any book promotions you use.

However, fiction also has some downsides:

- Difficulty coming up with interesting, engaging stories and characters
- Requires peace and quiet to concentrate (in my opinion anyway)
- Needs developmental editing and proof reading to ensure consistency and quality
- Can be difficult to make sales as some genres are extremely competitive and flooded with books
- Requires a lot of promotion or advertising to get your book seen and making money (some authors spend $5,000 or more a month on Amazon adverts but make back three or four times that investment)
- Physical book sales volumes are low, and you will rarely get expanded distribution orders unless your book is a big seller
- High-quality covers (required to make sales) can cost a lot of money, with some authors spending $1000 or more on a book cover

Fiction books can be any length from 20,000 words upwards. My recommendation is that if you are going over about 80,000 words, then split your book into multiple books. If you have one 150,000 word book, then you have one chance to grab a reader and one chance to earn money.

But, if you have two 75,000 word books or three 50,000 books, then you have more chances of grabbing readers. You also have the opportunity of people buying one of your books, enjoying it and buying the others, meaning you really capitalize on the sales you make. Your 150,000-word book may retail for $4.99, but what if your three 50,000 books sell for $2.99 each? For the same amount of words, you will be selling them for $8.97. This is a very good way to make more money and increase your popularity in Amazon by having more books available.

The length of the book is also determined by the genre. Heavy sci-fi or fantasy are often expected to be long (think Dune or Lord of the Rings) whereas romance or young adult are expected to be shorter.

A lot of people will decide on fiction because they do not feel they know enough about a subject to write nonfiction. As you proceed through this book, you will learn how to write a nonfiction book on any subject, even if you know nothing about it (believe me, I've done it when I worked as a ghost writer – I was asked to write about some very peculiar subjects).

Nonfiction has a lot of advantages too, such as:

- Relatively easy to make sales as people search Amazon for a solution to a problem and find your book
- Physical book sales often outweigh electronic book sales, meaning higher profits
- Physical books are often ordered via expanded distribution, which means bookshops, libraries, and educational establishments can order your books
- Very popular in the Kindle Unlimited program, meaning people can borrow your book and you get paid for every page their read
- Easy and quick to write
- Readers do not expect huge books, 20,000 to 50,000 words is usually sufficient for any nonfiction book
- Covers are relatively cheap; you can get a high-quality cover for under $10
- Most nonfiction is evergreen, meaning it will make sales for months or years. All you do is update the book every 12 to 18 months and ensure it is still relevant while adding any new information on the subject

But there are also disadvantages to nonfiction:

- It can be difficult to compete with celebrity or big name authors, although you may not be able to make their sales figures, you can certainly ride their coat-tails and benefit from people who want information on the subject but don't want to pay celebrity author prices
- Can be hard to successfully advertise as many book promotions are geared towards fiction authors

- Read through rates are poor because people tend to buy a nonfiction book to solve a problem. Once they've solved the problem, they do not require any additional books
- Some subjects can be difficult to write about
- Extra care must be taken not to infringe on copyright or plagiarize your content
- Can be harder to hit the big time with a few books

Even though read through rates are poor with nonfiction, it is worth writing a series if you can because you do get read through plus you can build a reputation and name within the niche which will help sales. If you can appear on multiple top 100 lists, then your potential readers will keep seeing your name and believe you are an established, well-known author.

Both types of books are good to write, and it is your decision which you approach. Writing fiction is a big subject, and I'm not going to tell you how to write a fiction book, so this book is going to focus more on nonfiction as it is easier for anyone to start writing and make money. However, all of the principles detailed for nonfiction work when writing fiction and will help ensure your book is successful.

Writing a Recipe Book

One of the most popular types of book is recipe books. Every celebrity has a recipe book in their name to go with their diet plan and exercise DVD. Celebrity chefs are all the rage, and they produce book after book of recipes that their fans buy.

Don't feel that the only people who can publish books are celebrities. Anyone can publish them, and there is a thriving market for reasonably priced recipe books. Picking a niche market works very well, plus seasonal recipe books also sell well at the appropriate seasons but sell nothing outside of this season.

Before we go any further, let me tell you where you stand on copyright. An ingredients list cannot be copyrighted, but the method or instructions can be copyrighted. This means that you can use recipes you find online as inspiration and can use the same ingredients and quantities in your book. What you cannot do is use the method ... but you can re-write it and make it 100% unique to you, and that is okay.

Recipe books sell well, but they do need pictures for them to become popular. Although you can use some stock photos here, it is better if you have pictures of the end result. You do not need step by step pictures for the recipes unless one is particularly complex. You also don't need a picture for every single recipe.

However, I strongly recommend that you make one or two of the recipes per chapter at home and take pictures of the final product. I'd also recommend taking pictures of each step because these can also be put into the recipe book to help add value and expand on the recipes. People love pictures, and if they can see what they end result will look like, then it helps them want to make the recipes and buy your book. In my experiments, I have found that recipe books with pictures sell far more than those without. I've found readers leave comments on books without pictures from people who say they wish there were more pictures.

Where you are unable to make the dishes, find some royalty free stock photos that you can use in your books. You may not be able to find the completed dish, but you can find an appealing picture of the ingredients which you can use.

For each recipe, write a short paragraph introducing the recipe, telling people how many servings the dish produces and other useful information about the recipe. Most of this can be gleaned from reading the original recipe and using some common sense. Try to think about substitutes that could be made, e.g. For a lasagna, you could substitute minced meat for a meat-free alternative to make the dish vegetarian.

Use both imperial and metric measurements in your recipe book because this helps widen the appeal, America uses the imperial measurement system whereas much of Europe uses the metric system. It takes a couple of minutes for each recipe to convert the measurements, just type the conversion into Google and it will give you the result, e.g. "4lb in kg" will convert 4 pounds into kilograms. By widening your appeal, you are making your book attractive to a wider market, which means potentially more sales. People can be put off a recipe book because the units of measurement are not one they are familiar with.

If you can include information about the number of servings the recipe makes, how long it takes to prepare and cook and so on, then you will help make your book more appealing to potential buyers.

Recipe books work best when they are focused on a specific subject, e.g. Thanksgiving, vegetarian, Chinese, Korean, crock pot and so on. Celebrity chefs can get away with a wider range of recipes, but keeping your book focused helps with sales. Remember that celebrity chef books are sold on the chef's name, whereas other recipe books are bought because of a need. People tend to buy recipe books for specific occasions or events.

The recipe book also needs to be a decent length. A book with a half dozen to a dozen recipes, unless they are out of this world, is going to struggle to sell. Where possible include the number of recipes in the title, e.g. "50 Amazing Korean Recipes". As you research the niche, you will see what type of books are selling and what you are competing with. This number helps with sales because people know how many recipes they are getting and it makes your book look more attractive than "Amazing Korean Recipes," where the reader doesn't know what they are getting.

When formatting your book, each recipe needs to start on a new page. This does make your book appear longer, but more importantly, it makes it clear where a recipe starts and finishes and makes it easier for the reader to concentrate on a single recipe. If you don't do this, you end up with the reader having to turn the page part way through the recipe or flick back and forth between pages. Either of these will annoy the reader and could result in negative reviews. Remember, you need to do everything possible to minimize the risk of negative reviews and maximize your chance of positive reviews.

Producing a recipe book is very easy to outsource. You can hire a data entry person from any of the outsourcing sites and get them to search the Internet and find the number of recipes you require. They will be happy with a couple of dollars an hour and should be able to find fifty different recipes in about eight to ten hours. Remember to give them precise instructions on what details you are expecting. You can then rewrite the recipes, or you can pay someone else to re-write them for you.

Recipe books are very popular, and when well written with some photographs, they can sell very well. They are easy to produce and are a good, perennial source of income because the recipes do not go out of date. However, be aware than some recipe books can be very seasonal in their sales, so don't bank on year round sales.

Writing a Children's Book

Children's books are another very popular genre, with high volumes of sales, and regular sales every year. These books have a long lifespan and do not tend to go out of date as every year there is a fresh, new group of children ready to be your target market.

With children's books, you need to write to a specific age group, and this means that the words and sentence structures you use need to be aimed at that age of child. You require a good understanding of what is necessary for each age group, and books that are not written at the right level will receive poor reviews and reduced sales.

There are resources online which will help you understand these different reading levels, and they vary from country to country. Once children reach the age of 11, they enter the Young Adult genre, which are full-length books but without violence, sex or drug use in. This genre is also extremely popular because many adults like to read young adult books because they are easy to read.

Children's books can either aim for an educational slant, with both fiction books or nonfiction books. Alternatively, you can go for just the fun reading, so long as your books are aimed at the right level.

One advantage of this type of book is you can let your imagination go wild. A very popular set of children's books are the stories of Captain Underpants, which are very peculiar, but kids love them. This gives you a lot more flexibility than with adult books, plus children's books are a lot more forgiving on the quality of the story line. Pretty much any story line is good enough so long as it keeps the child occupied and engaged for the duration.

One thing, though, that cannot suffer in a children's book is grammar and spelling. Unless you are using made up words, as Roald Dahl did, you have to ensure that every single word is spelled properly. Parents will not be forgiving if you are spelling words wrong! This can also mean that you need to publish separate US and UK versions of your book where your spelling and language is focused on each target market. This can significantly benefit sales as you can tap into both the American market and the rest of the world.

The younger the age of the child the book is aimed at, the shorter the book can be and the fewer words you need to use. In books aimed at younger children, you must use short words that will be within their vocabulary. Using the occasional word that pushes them up to the next vocabulary level is perfectly acceptable, but you shouldn't use words that are too complex as the child will not understand or enjoy the book.

Illustrations are equally important, more so with books aimed at a younger audience. Depending on the topic of your book, you may be able to use some stock photos, but otherwise, you are either going to have to illustrate the book yourself or hire someone to do it for you.

As the child grows older, so the need for illustrations is reduced, and they can become less frequent. In books such as the Captain Underpants books, there are illustrations throughout the book which add to the fun of the story, for the child, by helping them visualize what is going on.

If you are hiring a designer to create illustrations for you, then you must ensure that your contract with them ensures that all rights are transferred to you for use as you see fit. You should also ensure that they are not going to try and sell the pictures on to anyone else. If you are buying pre-made illustrations, then you want to ensure you have exclusive rights to them. This will cost a bit more but does ensure that your books remain unique.

One big advantage of children's books is that they can be very quick to write. You can write one in a day, easily, depending on the market you are aiming for. These also sell well without a huge amount of promotion but will benefit from advertising to help get the word out. You will benefit from creating a social media presence, ideally Facebook, Twitter, Instagram, and Pinterest so that you can connect with the parents of your target market and notify them of new releases or promotions.

If you are happy to write children's books, then they are very profitable, and you can easily publish a lot of books in a single year. There is a definite talent to creating these books, and you will see more physical sales than electronic sales. These are also worth putting into Amazon's expanded distribution for physical books as you can find schools ordering your books for their pupils.

WRITING A FICTION BOOK

Fiction is very profitable, and many authors dive into fiction because there is a lot of potential to make money here. It is possible to hit four figures a month as an Indie author with a single fiction book, and you could do that too.

Fiction tends to be very cut throat, and without plenty of promotion, books disappear. Many authors tear their hair out with the cost of promotion and the time it takes to push their books, but it does pay off. As so many people delve into fiction writing, it is highly competitive, and your book needs to stand out from the crowd.

For fiction to be profitable, you will need a series of books. Anything from a trilogy upwards will work because when readers finish one book, if they have enjoyed it, they will naturally look for the next book in the series. If it is priced correctly, then they will buy then and there.

However, a couple of caveats. Firstly, your book has to be good. If your book does not engage the reader, then they are unlikely to finish it or want to move on to the next book. Secondly, your book must be a complete story. Some authors will finish a story halfway through and split it into a second book. If your readers feel you are trying to force them to buy the next book, they may get upset, but if your story is complete then they will be eager to move on to the next one.

Fiction sells very well in electronic form, though physical book sales are quite slow for most Indie authors. The majority of fiction readers, particularly those in any of the science fiction, romance (all types) and crime genres read voraciously, often finishing multiple books every month. They tend to read on an electronic device and will buy multiple books from an author they like.

My wife has several favorite authors, and she has bought every book they have written, and one of the writers has written over 50 books! This is typical behavior from a reader, so reader loyalty is something you need to work on. They do not tend to buy physical books because once they have read a book, they are unlikely to return to the book again.

This does not mean you shouldn't publish your book as a paperback, in fact, the opposite applies, you must publish your book in both electronic and paperback format.

Why?

Because too many authors only publish in electronic format and readers associate books that are only available as eBooks with being poor quality or self-published. Books that are published in both formats are seen as more trustworthy, and many people will assume traditionally published, so therefore of higher quality (yes, I know that isn't always true, but it is a perception in the mind of your reader).

Publishing in both formats gives you more credibility in the eyes of your readers, and even though you may not sell many paperbacks, it will boost your Kindle sales. If your book does do well and becomes a bestseller, then the physical book sales will pick up and may even be bought by bookshops and libraries, further increasing your profit and popularity. Having a physical book also means you can do book signings and other promotions which involve you giving away copies of your book.

Pricing

Fiction books are harder to price as you are competing with a lot of traditionally published books, that even in their electronic form sell for upwards of $5.

Where you publish your book will depend on your strategy, and this is different for everyone. I would suggest that you analyze the genre you are writing in and see what other authors, particularly Indie authors, are doing. Look at the bestselling books in your chosen categories and see how they are priced as it will give you a good idea of what your readers are willing to pay for books.

Some people will price the first book in a series at 99c, $2.99 or even free to hook people into the series. To price your book free you need to publish it for free elsewhere and then ask Amazon to price match it. They do not like books to be published for no cost. This book needs to be outstanding because then people will buy more books in the series. The rest of the books are priced at $2.99, $4.99 or higher, though be aware there may well be a price ceiling in your genre.

How you price the book depends on what other people are doing in your niche as if everyone else is pricing at 99c and you price yours at $4.99 you may struggle to sell in light of the cheaper competition. Research is required for you to determine what is the best approach for you and the genre you are writing in.

Book Covers

With fiction, the book cover is even more important than it is for nonfiction. People genuinely judge a book by its cover, and if your cover doesn't leap out, grab the reader by the eyes and drag them in, you will struggle to make sales.

Although nonfiction book covers can be very cheap (you'll learn this further on in this book), good fiction covers are more expensive. You are looking to spend a minimum of $100 and up to $1000 for a professional, unique cover that grabs attention.

Again, you need to research the competition to look at what the components of a bestselling book in your genre are. Go through the top 100 bestseller list and look at which books are most successful and what they have on their cover. Their covers will have similarities in style, content and color which you need to mimic (but not copy) to get the attention of your readers. People expect covers in a genre to conform to a theme and in general, the best sellers will. Occasionally a cover will buck the trend, but that is the exception rather than the rule.

Tropes

Most genres have what are referred to by authors as 'tropes.' These are basically expectations of content, i.e. What the reader is going to experience in the book.

For example, dystopian future books will, in the majority of cases, all have a female heroine who is a teenager or just into their twenties. They'll have lost a parent or both their parents tragically and then fight back against the system, usually against an older male protagonist.

Every genre has their tropes, and it is important that you have a deep understanding of these because your readers expect to find them in your book. Again, occasionally books will go against this theme, but it is rare.

Look through the bestselling books, ideally, read a couple of them, and determine what consistent themes there are in the books. You can usually get the gist either from the blurb about the book or the look inside feature on Amazon which allows you to read the first few pages of a book. It is worth investing in Kindle Unlimited for a couple of months so that you can read some of the books in your chosen niche and understand these tropes.

Make sure you include all of the required tropes in your book. Readers like books that are comfortable and relaxing to read. If they pick up a book in a genre and it goes completely against the grain of the genre, then it pushes them out of their comfort zone and is no longer a relaxing, mind clearing read. It will put readers off and could lead to negative reviews as people vent their frustration at not getting what they expect.

Fiction is a great way forwards for some people, and if you want to write fiction, then I'd say go for it. I would recommend you look for some creative writing classes, either locally or online as that will help you produce better quality books. There are many free online sites such as coursera and edx which offer university level courses in grammar, English language and creative writing. These are definitely worth taking as they will help improve your writing.

If a popular author in your genre has released a book about how to write fiction, such as Stephen King's book on the subject, then you need to buy that book and read it because you will get a lot of useful information to create a bestseller in your genre. Unless there is specific information you require, you do not need to go out and buy hundreds of books or pay for expensive training programs. There is a lot of very good quality information out there for free.

KDP & CREATESPACE EXPLAINED

There are lots of potential platforms for you to publish on, which we will discuss in the next chapter. For now, you are going to gain a better understanding of Amazon's self-publishing options, CreateSpace and Kindle Direct Publishing.

Kindle Direct Publishing (KDP)

This is found at http://kdp.amazon.com and is where you publish your books to the Kindle platform. It is free to sign up to, and there is no cost whatsoever for you to publish a book. Amazon will pay you a commission, based on the sales price minus some costs, on each sale that you make.

When publishing on KDP, you can create a paperback version of your book through CreateSpace at the end of the process, though expect this to be stopped soon. I would not recommend taking this option because the formatting is dreadful and your printed book looks thoroughly unprofessional. If you are publishing a paperback, get the book formatted correctly and publish it directly through the CreateSpace website. Amazon will automatically link the paperback with the e-book, but if they don't then a simple email to their support team will get the two versions of the book linked together.

Recently, at the time of writing, Amazon has introduced the ability to publish paperbacks directly through the KDP program. This appears to be the future, as far as Amazon is concerned, and will, at some time, replace CreateSpace publishing. Keep an eye on this because it could be worth using in the future. At present though, there is no facility to access expanded distribution markets, which a lot of authors like and profit from. However, it is likely to be added in the future once Amazon has fully decided what to do with this new publishing platform.

Before you publish your book, you need to write it using a word processor of your choice. It's up to you which you use, I use Microsoft Word because I am familiar with it, but you may prefer a different tool.

Write your book in normal page size format. Remember that there is such a wide range of e-readers, ranging from a small cell phone to a tablet to dedicated e-reader like a Kindle. Because of this, it is impossible for you to format your book so it looks perfect on all readers. Write it in normal page format, and it will look fine in the readers, you get a chance to preview it before publishing anyway.

I won't walk you through the publishing process as this does change regularly. What I will do is highlight a few of the key points you need to be aware of.

I would recommend that you write your description for your book on your computer and then copy and paste it into your book listing. The box provided for you to enter your description is rather small, making typing directly into it very hard. You have just 4000 characters in which to impress your readers with the need to buy your book. More on this, known as the blurb, later in this book.

Keywords

You will need to enter some keywords into your book listing. These are terms that people will type into Amazon when looking for your book. They can be a single word, or they can be a phrase.

The best way to do this is to go to Amazon and select Kindle or Books from the drop down menu next to the search bar. This lets you just search those categories for keywords. Now type in the first few letters of the subject of your book and Amazon will come up with some helpful suggestions for you. These can be your keywords, though remember you can only use seven, so pick the best! With CreateSpace, you can only use five keywords and are limited in the number of characters you can use.

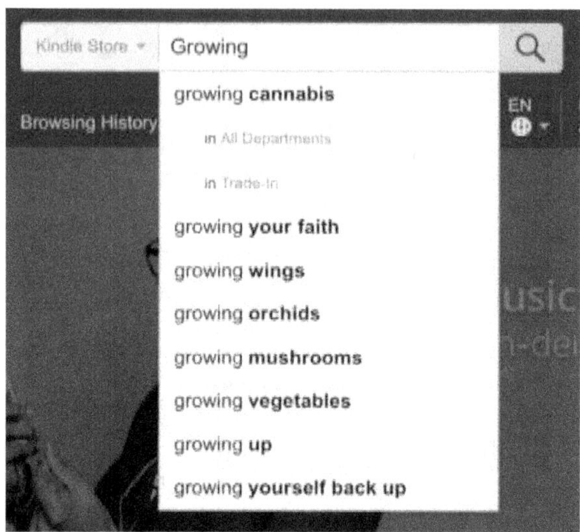

You can see from this example, I've typed the word 'Growing' in and selected the Kindle Store. It has now suggested the most popular keywords in that category. If I keep entering more letters, I can narrow down the suggestions further to my specific subject.

Keywords are quite important to your book because they influence how people find it. It tells Amazon the main subject areas of your book, and it can then display your book to other people who are searching for information on the subject. Always make sure you enter all seven permitted keywords, and that they are relevant to the content of your book. Amazon takes a dim view of spamming, so avoid doing anything that could be construed as spamming the keywords.

Book Categories

Another important consideration is the categories. You can choose up to two categories, and you must use both. Amazon will add you to other categories once it works out what your book is about and you can always ask Amazon to add your book to additional categories (raise a support ticket with them) later on when it is selling.

Research popular books in your niche and look at the categories they are listed in. You will find this in the listing for a book, under the product details section. Write them all down and then look at that specific category to see who your competition is.

Product details

File Size: 3085 KB
Print Length: 224 pages
Publisher: Storey Publishing, LLC; 2nd Rev and Updated ed. edition (January 2, 1998)
Publication Date: January 2, 1998
Sold by: Amazon Digital Services LLC
Language: English
ASIN: B004A7YINO
Text-to-Speech: Enabled
X-Ray: Enabled
Word Wise: Not Enabled
Lending: Not Enabled
Screen Reader: Supported
Enhanced Typesetting: Enabled
Amazon Best Sellers Rank: #9,463 Paid in Kindle Store (See Top 100 Paid in Kindle Store)
> #2 in Kindle Store > Kindle eBooks > Crafts, Hobbies & Home > Gardening & Horticulture > **Herbs**
> #3 in Kindle Store > Kindle eBooks > Crafts, Hobbies & Home > Gardening & Horticulture > **Vegetables**
> #4 in Kindle Store > Kindle eBooks > Crafts, Hobbies & Home > Gardening & Horticulture > **Techniques**

You can see this book is ranking very well in its categories. Go through the top ten to twenty books in your chosen niche and make a note of all the categories that the books are in. You can also have a quick read of the reviews of each book and note any positive or negative points about the book. You are looking for what the reader liked because you want to include that in your book, and what they felt was missing or wrong, so you can avoid making that mistake. This information itself is worth its weight in gold and will help you create a high-quality book.

Once you have done this, you will have a list of categories that you could put your book in. Check the categories on Amazon to see how many other books are in each one, because it is easier to rank well and get noticed in a smaller category. Categories with more books in can be very competitive and difficult to both rank in and make sales.

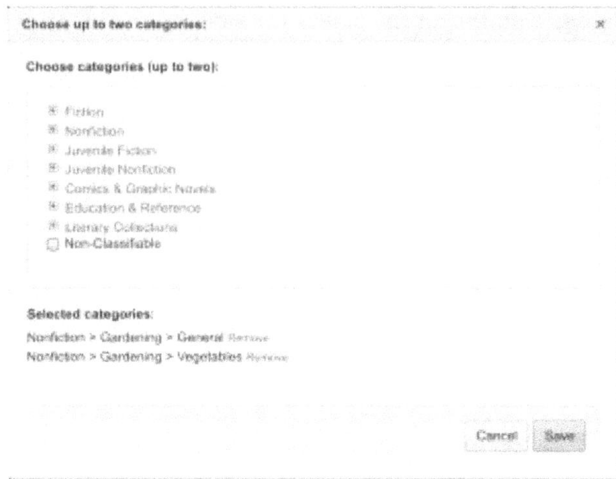

Select the categories that you feel best match your book, and you have a good chance of ranking in. Remember, after the book has sold a few copies you can email Amazon to ask them to add your book to other categories.

Author Details

You are given the option of entering the author name plus details of any contributors. Unless you are using a pen name, you should put your name in here. Make sure how you enter your name is how it appears on your book covers. My book covers all say 'Jason Johns' so in the author field I always put my full name, rather than an initial and my surname.

You can also enter information about anyone who has contributed to the book. This is useful if you have co-authored the book or are producing a box set with multiple authors. You do not need to enter anyone's name unless they hold copyright in some form to your book. This means that if you have hired someone to research recipes for you, there is no need to enter their name as a contributor. If you have hired someone to rewrite the recipes for you, then they also do not need to be entered as a contributor because they hold no claim to copyright on the book.

However, if you have collaborated with someone to write a book, then they have to be listed, for example, if you have a co-written it with a photographer or illustrator. If you have bought publishing rights to pictures or illustrations, they do not need adding as a contributor.

You can see the variety of contributors available to you. In the majority of cases, it is just you who is the author, and there is no requirement to add any other contributors.

Publishing Rights

There are two options when publishing on Amazon. You either hold full rights to the book, or you are publishing a public domain work, e.g. Aesop's fables.

Although Amazon allows you to sell public domain works, you need to ensure the books are actually public domain and Amazon can ask for proof.

They will not publish a public domain work which has not been significantly changed. If you are just taking public domain works and republishing them, then your book will be rejected. Amazon states books must be differentiated, which means:

- A unique translation of the book (into a different language)
- Significant annotations added, such as a study guide, critique and so on
- A minimum of ten new illustrations added to the book

You can read the full requirements from Amazon at https://kdp.amazon.com/help/topic/A2OHLJURFVK57Q?ref_=_pd and understand exactly what needs to be done so you can publish a public domain work.

Personally, I never bother with public domain works but prefer to write my own which have more earning potential and less chance of conflict with Amazon. The last thing I want to do is annoy the 1000lb gorilla that pays me a commission every month!

Select the option that best suits you, in most cases, you will hold the necessary publishing rights.

Age & Grade Range

If you are publishing children's books, then you have to fill in this information. If you are publishing towards an adult market, then this information is not required by Amazon.

This gives readers the information they need to understand what age of child the book is suitable for. You can either select the age range of children the book will suit, and you can also select the school grade that the book is suitable for. Select the right age ranges based on your research and writing or ignore this if you have written a book aimed at adults. Even on an adult book, you can enter this information if you want to, though it isn't required.

Publishing Your Manuscript

Once you move on to the second page, you can now upload your manuscript. Make sure it is one of the formats Amazon will accept and once it has uploaded and processed, preview it using the option presented to you further down the screen.

Document formats accepted are:

- Microsoft Word (DOC or DOCX)
- HTML (ZIP, HTM or HTML)
- MOBI
- EPUB
- Rich Text Format (RTF)
- Plain Text (TXT)
- Adobe PDF (PDF)

- Kindle Package Format (KPF)

Which you use will depend on the word processor and your preference. I always use Microsoft Word format as that is what I use to write my books and involves the least messing around. If you have trouble getting your book to display properly, try changing it to a Microsoft Word format, a MOBI or an EPUB as that can solve many display issues. Sometimes there can be issues displaying pictures formatted correctly, and I have found that using an HTML file format can make the pictures display properly.

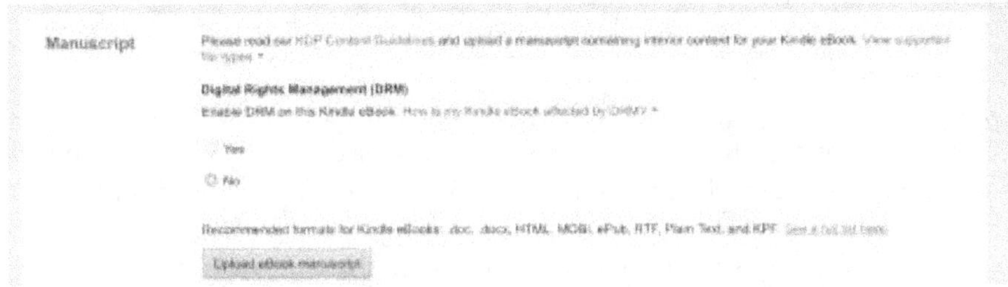

When uploading your manuscript, you also have the option of setting Digital Rights Management (DRM). This supposedly prevents copying of your book, but to be fair, it causes more trouble than it is worth.

Anyone who wants to copy your book will be able to regardless of whether or not DRM is enabled. For those honest users, it ends up causing them hassle for a variety of reasons, which can then mean they struggle to read your book. The general feeling amongst most authors, including myself, is to leave this switched off. It isn't going to help you make sales and can hinder your book.

Kindle Ebook Cover
You now have to upload your cover. We'll talk about covers later on, but you can either upload it in JPG or TIFF format or use Amazon's online cover creator.

I strongly recommend that you upload a pre-made cover. Although the online cover creator is powerful, the covers it creates look a little amateurish. This is going to impact your sales negatively. I recommend you hire a good designer and upload the finished product directly.

You can read all about Amazon's cover guidelines through this link, https://kdp.amazon.com/help/topic/A2J0TRG6OPX0VM.

Kindle Ebook ISBN

Finally, you may enter an ISBN. This is not required for electronic books, but you may have an ISBN if your book is published elsewhere or through a traditional publisher. You can also enter a publishers name here if you have a publisher.

KDP Select Program

You can choose to enroll your book into the KDP select program, which means it must be exclusive to Amazon for 90 days. We'll talk more about this in the next chapter.

Territories

This is where you can set your book to be distributed worldwide or in specific countries. Most of the time you will choose worldwide distribution, but in some cases, you may choose to distribute your book in specific countries.

If your book is written in a language other than English, then you may want to only distribute it in countries that speak that language. This applies for translations you've had done of your book too.

If you do not have rights to distribute your book outside of a specific country, then you will choose the countries you do have the rights for.

Royalty and Pricing

This is the part which can be confusing for most people, and pricing will be discussed fully later in this book.

When your book is priced at less than $2.99, you have to sell your book at a 35% commission. The upside of this is that you do not incur a delivery charge, but the downside is you earn less. If you are pricing your book at $0.99, then you have to set your commission rate to 35%.

Once your book is priced at $2.99 or higher, you can set the royalty rate to 70%, which has a significant impact increasing your earnings. You will get charged for the delivery of your eBook, based on the size of the book in megabytes (MB). The larger the book, the more you will get charged.

The cost depends on which country you are in and works out at an amount multiplied the number of megabytes, rounded up to the nearest kilobyte.

Delivery Costs are equal to the number of megabytes we determine your Digital Book file contains, multiplied by the Delivery Cost rate listed below.

Amazon.com: US $0.15/MB
Amazon.ca: CAD $0.15/MB
Amazon.com.br: R$0.30/MB
Amazon.co.uk: UK £0.10/MB
Amazon.de: €0,12/MB
Amazon.fr: €0,12/MB
Amazon.es: €0,12/MB
Amazon.in: INR ₹7/MB
Amazon.it: €0,12/MB
Amazon.nl: €0,12/MB
Amazon.co.jp: ¥1/MB
Amazon.com.mx: MXN $1/MB
Amazon.com.au: AUD $0.15/MB

We will round file sizes up to the nearest kilobyte. The minimum Delivery Cost for a Digital Book will be US$0.01 for sales in US Dollars, INR₹1 for sales in Indian Rupees, CAD$0.01 for sales in CAD Dollars, £0.01 for sales in GB Pounds, ¥1 in JPY, R$0.01 for sales in Brazilian Reais, MXN$1 for sales in Mexican Pesos, AUD$0.01 for sales in Australian Dollars, and €0.01 for sales in Euros, regardless of file size. For sales in JPY, we will not deduct any Delivery Cost for books 10 MB or greater.

If your book has a lot of pictures in it, then this cost can quickly eat away at your profits, making your book a poor earner. You can reduce the commission rate to 35%, which eliminates the delivery charge, which could be an option with some books. However, you can compress the pictures in your book, which we'll talk about in the section on pictures shortly.

Enter your list price and select your commission rate. Amazon will work out and display the amount you will earn per book. Once you have done this, you can click the link that says "Base all marketplaces on this price." This will set the price for the remaining countries based on the price of your book in US dollars.

Then go through all of the other countries and check the pricing. Sometimes it will convert your $2.99 book into a price of something peculiar like 4.58. Although this is a fair translation of the price based on the exchange rate, it can impact your sales. There is a whole school of thought based on pricing and what numbers to end your prices in. It's worth looking up if you are interested, or in need of a good night's sleep!

Most people are used to buying products that end in a 9, though many marketers claim that ending your price with a seven grabs attention and boosts sales. When you buy most items, they are 1.99 or 9.99 or 99.99, they all end in a 9. When your book is priced ending in a number other than nine then it can impact sales. Sometimes it is worth pricing your book to a more 'normal' figure such as 4.49 or 4.99.

Check the prices for each of the countries listed and change the prices where required. Each time you change the price, you can calculate what your earnings will be.

Matchbook

This is an option whereby people who buy your physical book can then either buy the electronic version for a lower price or for free.

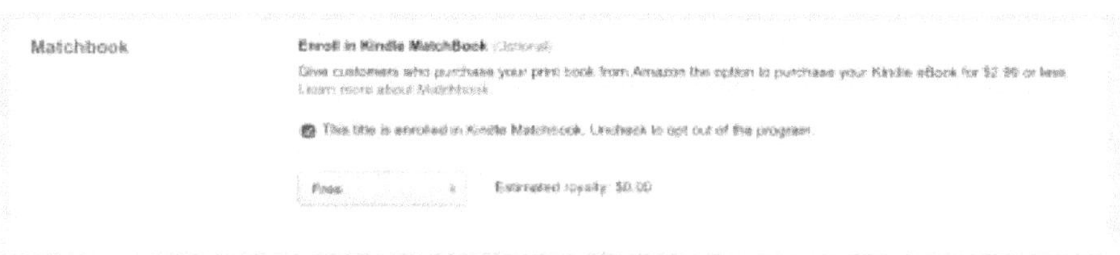

Which you do is entirely up to you. My approach is to offer people a free download of my electronic book when they buy the physical book. This allows people to get a full-color version of my book for free as the printing costs of full-color books with Amazon are prohibitive.

This can be a nice bonus for your readers and help you make sales of physical books. If your main market is electronic books, then you can ignore this section.

Book Lending
Kindle owners can lend books they buy to their friends or family for up to 14 days. This has no impact on your earnings, but one advantage of permitting lending is that you can increase your market reach and, if your books are good, the people who borrow them may well buy a copy of the book for themselves, read it on KDP select or buy other books you have written.

I would recommend turning this on because it gives you an opportunity to expand awareness of yourself as an author.

Finally, you need to agree to the Terms and Conditions and publish your book. It can take anything up to 72 hours for your book to go live, compared to under 24 hours on CreateSpace. Usually, it is quicker than that, with most books made live in 36 to 48 hours.

Once your book is published, you can then enter your book into CreateSpace or publish it as a Kindle paperback.

CreateSpace

CreateSpace is Amazon's print on demand service for paperback books, CD's, DVD's and video downloads, though the latter two may disappear in coming months as Amazon's video service takes off.

There is no cost involved in adding your book to CreateSpace and Amazon will sell the book on their site plus permit expanded distribution to libraries, book shops, and educational establishments.

Before you start, you will need to decide what size your book will be. Amazon offers a wide variety of sizes for your books, which gives you a lot of flexibility plus the print quality is good. Some people are not overly happy with the print copy, but without spending a lot of money on a different print on demand service, this is very good. The majority of readers will be completely satisfied with your book, and you are very unlikely to get any complaints about print quality. The books are printed to library quality.

The book trim sizes offered are:

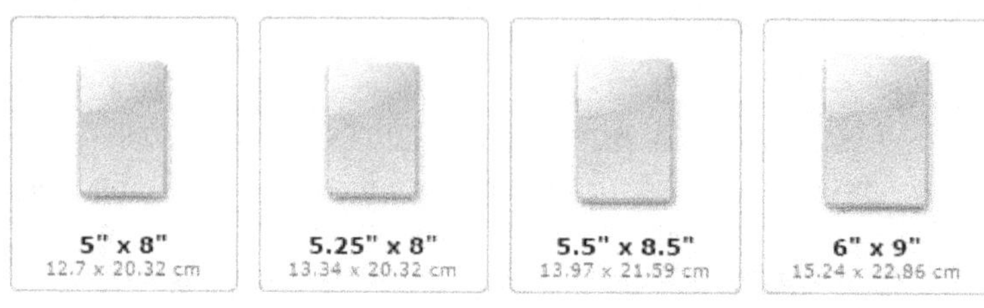

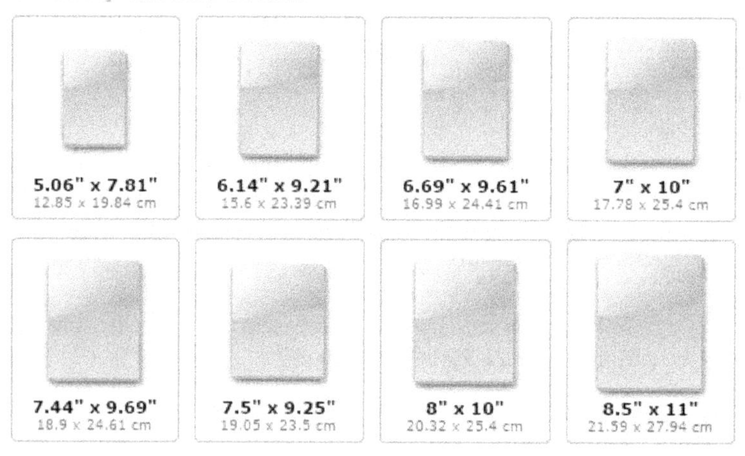

You do have the option to select your own trim size if you want, but you need to be aware of the limitations of doing so. When you select anything other than the industry standard trim sizes, it can limit your distribution options as some expanded distribution opportunities will not be available to you.

Your book needs to be specifically formatted for CreateSpace because buyers of physical books will get upset if the book is poorly formatted and are much more likely to leave a negative review.

Although you can publish directly to CreateSpace from KDP, the formatting is dreadful. It is much better to download a template for your chosen trim size and use that. Amazon provides basic templates for all book trim sizes here:

https://forums.createspace.com/en/community/docs/DOC-1323.

There is also a link in there for Amazon's submission guidelines, which can be worth a read.

Much of the information required to publish on CreateSpace is the same as for publishing on KDP. You can re-use your description from publishing on KDP. Enter your book title, author name and any other information required.

ISBN Numbers

When publishing a paperback, you need an ISBN, which is a unique identifier for your book.

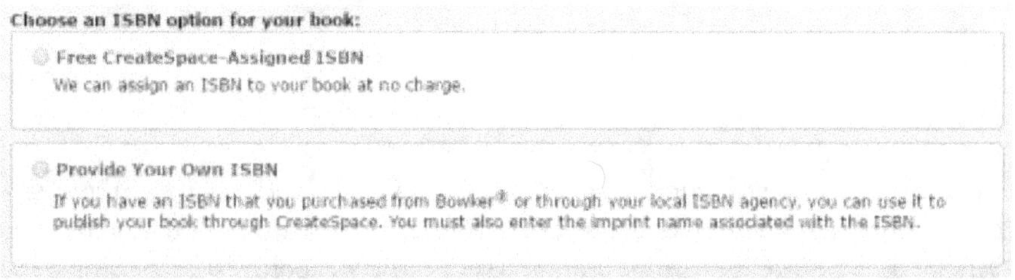

You can buy your own ISBN numbers if you prefer, or you can use a free ISBN provided by Amazon.

If your book is published elsewhere and you already have an ISBN, then you will use that, otherwise, use the free ISBN provided by Amazon. There is no requirement for you to purchase your own ISBN numbers.

Should you change the cover, size or title of your book then you will need to re-publish your book as it will require a new ISBN.

Interior

Submitting the interior of your book is easy, you just upload your prepared template file to CreateSpace. If you prefer, you can hire Amazon's professional design services, which starts at $199, though you can find outsourcers elsewhere who will format your book for you.

Choose your interior type and paper color too.

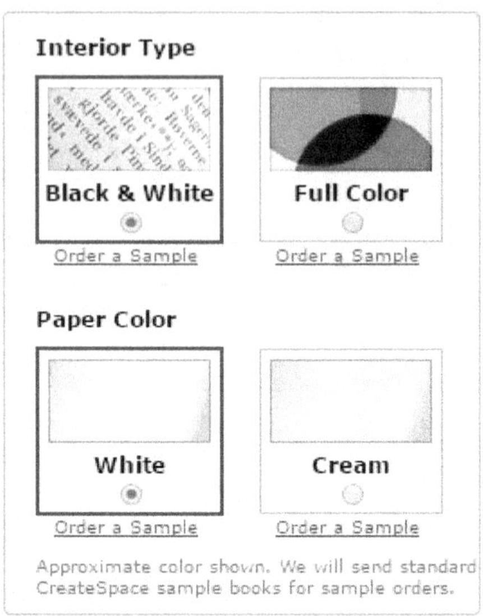

Be aware that if you choose full color, then it does add significantly to the cost of printing and can make your book very uncompetitive. I publish mainly nonfiction, and most of my books have a lot of color photographs in. Unfortunately, the cost of printing means that my books have to be priced too high to sell for me to make any profit. My paperbacks are printed in black and white, and I state at the front of the book that buyers can get the full-color Kindle version for free.

Let's imagine we are going to produce a 6x9" book with 150 pages so that I can show you the difference in costs.

Printing this as a full-color book means I have to sell it at $18.99 to make $0.04 in royalties! Through the expanded distribution network, I would get -$3.76 at that price!

However, printing the book in black and white and still pricing it at $18.99 would give me $8.74 in royalties through Amazon's website and $4.94 through the expanded distribution network.

You can see the massive difference in cost which, unfortunately, makes printing full-color books uncompetitive through CreateSpace.

Cover

Next, you need to upload your book cover. Firstly, choose whether you want a glossy or matte cover. I always choose glossy myself, but some people may prefer matte.

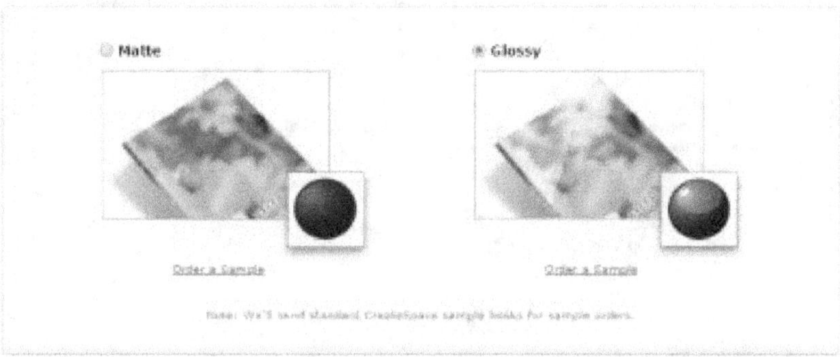

After this, you can decide to use the CreateSpace cover designer, hire Amazon to produce your cover for you (starting at $399) or upload your own cover in PDF format.

I would strongly recommend the latter option. The online cover designer is okay, but the resulting book covers just do not look professional enough, in my opinion, to make sales. Hire a cover designer, more on that later, to create a print ready cover and upload that. The results will be better, and you are likely to make more sales.

Complete Setup & Review

After you have completed all of the above, your book is ready to be submitted to Amazon for approval. Complete the setup and then when it is approved, review your book.

You can use the online viewer, download a PDF or order a printed copy of your book. The latter will cost you money, and if you are outside of the USA, it can take some time to arrive unless you pay a lot for postage.

I use the online viewer and go through the book, page by page, checking the formatting is correct, the header and footer are in the right place, the table of contents looks okay, the pictures are in the right position and so on. I don't proof read it in this viewer, that is done before publication, but I check the layout so I can see what the book will look like when it is printed.

Channels

Next, you need to choose your distribution options. Firstly, you can select the channels, but you cannot select the additional channels until you have chosen BISAC codes in the Description section.

You will automatically have Amazon.com, Amazon Europe and CreateSpace store selected as these are the default options.

There is also the option to distribution via CreateSpace Direct, which is selected by default and then you can choose for your book to be distributed to bookstores and online retailers as well as libraries and academic institutions.

Both of these purchase your book at a lower price, so your commissions are lower. Depending on how you have priced your book, you can end up with a minimal commission. From my experiences, nonfiction books do better in expanded distribution channels than fiction books.

Once you have selected your BISAC category, then you must return here and select the other distribution channels, if you are planning on using them.

Be aware that these expanded distribution channels buy your books at a discounted price, meaning your commission is lower. This pushes up the price of your book, and you can find, in some instances, that your regular sales price becomes too high when using these additional channels. If this is the case, you need to determine whether the higher price is worth the benefits of the expanded distribution channels.

Pricing

Setting your price is very important as it has to be affordable, so people will buy your book. Amazon will help by calculating the royalties for you when you enter prices.

You can choose to base the prices of the UK and Europe on the US dollar price, or you can set the price to make it a little bit more user-friendly but unticking the box. When you change the price, click 'calculate' which will update the royalty amounts shown on the right-hand site.

Keep an eye on the royalty amount for the expanded distribution channel as you test different prices. This can end up being very low or even a negative figure, depending on the pricing of your book.

Cover Finish

Next, you get to choose the cover finish. There are two choices, matte or glossy. Most people choose glossy, but in some cases, you may want matte.

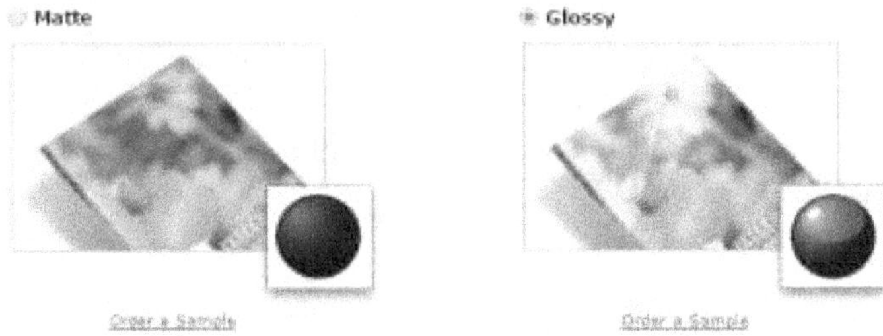

Description

Next, you enter the description, you can re-use your Kindle description here.

The BISAC category needs choosing next. This can be difficult finding the right category, but spend some time finding the category that best suits your book.

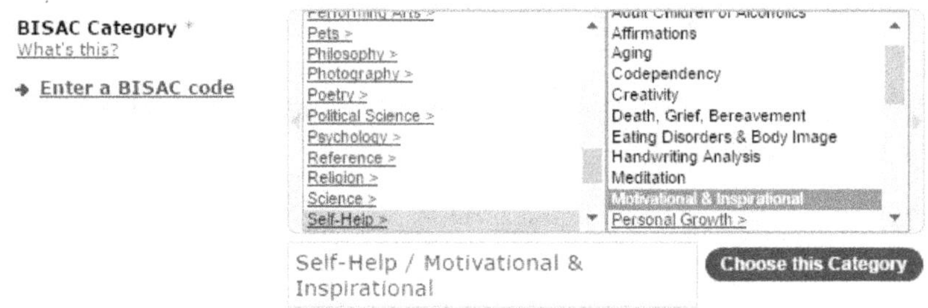

It can be a bit tricky to navigate and a little frustrating, but with some patience, you will find a suitable category.

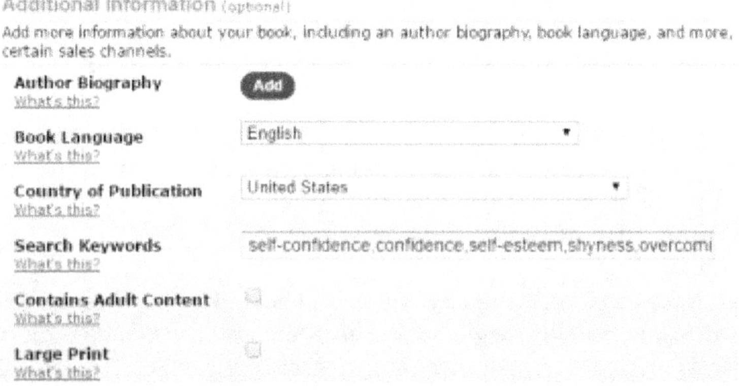

Finally, you have a few more options to enter.

I strongly recommend you include an author bio. This is some additional words which will appear at the bottom of your book listing and provide the reader with more information about you. This is important because big name authors all have an author biography. The small fry don't bother with this, so by entering a biography, you are instantly setting yourself apart from the crowd.

Perhaps most importantly, it gives you a chance to connect with your reader on a personal level and tell them a part of your story. This can help with sales as people feel they get to know you.

The book language and country of publication are self-explanatory.

Keywords are important too, and you can re-use those you chose for your Kindle book. However, you are only allowed five keywords, and there is a character limitation of 25 characters. Keywords must be separated by commas, and the character limit will mean you may have to re-think a couple of keywords.

If your book contains adult content, then you must select the next box. If you do not, there is a chance Amazon could get unhappy with you and suspend your book. This is to help Amazon protect minors from inappropriate content, and they will take action if you fail to check this box when your book contains adult content.

Finally, you can select Large Print if your book is a large print edition.

Once you are done, you click publish, wait for Amazon to tell you that your book is okay, then you review the book again. This is done either through an online viewer, or you order a copy of the book, which will take time for it to arrive and so delays the publication of your book. Which you do is entirely up to you.

Which to Choose

Most people are going to publish on Kindle as it is quick and easy to do. Some people will then choose to publish their book as paperback either through the Kindle publishing service or through CreateSpace.

The downside of CreateSpace is that it is not very cost effective to produce full-color books. There are alternative print on demand publishers, such as Ingram Spark, but they charge for setting up a book and then charge again every time you make a change plus there is a yearly fee for keeping your book on file. Books from Ingram Spark can be made available to buy on Amazon and are eligible for Amazon prime.

Which you choose is entirely up to you and will depend on your book and your publishing strategy.

At the moment, CreateSpace is the only option if you want access to the expanded distribution channels. However, not everyone will want these and so publishing a paperback through Kindle can be a better option. It is very simple to set up and publish and if you just want to publish your book, worth doing.

Amazon is the behemoth of publishing online, but there are many other places you can publish your book, as you are about to find out.

BENEFITS OF KDP SELECT VS. PUBLISHING WIDE

When publishing a book on the Kindle, you have a choice to enroll your book into the KDP Select program. This allows readers to borrow your book, rather than buy it, as part of the Kindle Unlimited program (a monthly subscription).

You are then paid a small amount, between $0.040 and $0.055, for every page read. The figure varies from month to month, depending on how much Amazon decides to pay. This is usually announced during the second or occasionally the third week of the month via an email to your registered email address. However, most author forums will be alive with discussion as soon as the announcement is made.

This can be a very good earner for popular books, though if you decide to enroll your book, then it must be exclusive to Amazon for a period of 90 days. Every time you enroll your book, you are enrolling it for a 90 day period. During those 90 days, your book cannot be made available through any other bookseller, except CreateSpace. You can remove your book at any time, but you need to wait until the end of the 90 day period before you can sell your book elsewhere.

KDP Select can be extremely lucrative, with people earning thousands of dollars a month from it. Some authors get millions of page reads a month; others get thousands. However, you may decide that this isn't for you because you would rather sell books on other platforms. If you do not enroll your book in KDP Select, then you can make your book available through Barnes & Noble, iBooks, and other sites.

For some books, this can make more money and help you expand your reader base. For others, they won't make that much money. You need to look at these two different choices and decide which is for you.

Typically, the majority of your book sales will come from Amazon, so it makes sense to enroll your book and to make money from people borrowing your book. However, you may look at having your book exclusive to Amazon as meaning you have all your eggs in one basket. This means that should Amazon disappear overnight, which is highly unlikely, or they shut your account down for some reason, you have lost your business as all your books are in one place.

This is another personal decision, and it is entirely up to you which you choose. You must consider that Amazon has been around since 1995, and is highly unlikely to disappear anytime soon. Providing your follow Amazon's terms of service and your books are good quality and unique, you are unlikely to find your account suspended.

However, although you can earn some money from KDP, and for some people, it is a lot of money, it may be you can make more money from 'wide' distribution through channels other than Amazon.

When you first publish your book, put it into the KDP Select program and see how well it performs. After 90 days, look at the amount of money it has earned through page reads.

If you are happy with this, then leave it in KDP Select. If you feel it hasn't performed very well, then take it out of KDP Select and choose wide distribution. Later on, in this book, we will talk about some services you can use which means you don't have to visit every single retailer to list your book. Some authors will leave their book in KDP Select for the first 90 days before removing it to go wide.

This is a personal decision. There is no right or wrong answer, only what works best for you. At the time of writing, all my books are enrolled in KDP Select as they bring in some good money from this. However, a few books are not making as much as I think they could and they are going to be taken out of KDP Select soon and tested on wide distribution to see what they can earn from other channels. If they do not perform as expected, then I will return them to KDP Select.

By constantly monitoring your books and testing new methods, you can maximize your earnings. Start with KDP Select, see what results you get and then test wide distribution if you feel it could do better.

BOOKS ARE JUDGED BY THEIR COVER

Your book cover is absolutely vital in ensuring you make sales. A poor cover will cripple your book and make it almost impossible to sell. It is imperative that you have a high quality cover that entices your reader to click on your book to find out more.

Time and time again I see an author bemoaning their lack of sales only to look at their book cover and see something that is amateurish, not related to their niche or of dreadful quality. If your book cover isn't right, then you are going to face an uphill struggle to make sales. The book cover is one of the three components that sell your book for you, so it has to be the best you can get.

Don't think you can create a cover now and then change it in the future when your book is making money. Without a good cover, you may struggle to make the sales that give your book a future! It is worth spending as much as you can comfortably afford now to get a good cover to give your book the best start in life. Yes, you can change it later on, and people often do to revive flagging sales, but be aware of how important the cover is in making sales.

Do It Yourself vs. Hire a Professional

When a lot of people write their first book, they are on a very tight budget. There is no money coming in, and it can be hard to justify the cost of a cover. At this point, some people decide to create their own book cover.

Stop.

Think.

Are you a good graphics designer? Can you produce a good quality cover?

Do you know the technical specifications for a book cover?

If the answer is no, then stop right now and hire someone. Too many authors make the mistake of creating their own cover, and the cover is boring, looks amateurish or unprofessional and so does not entice people to buy.

Remember that your cover is a massive part of your sales process. In most cases, it is the first thing that your potential reader will see. They look at the cover, then read the title and then, if they are interested, will click and read the description. The cover is absolutely vital, and its importance should never be underestimated.

You can do the cover yourself, and some authors do. However, if you are not gifted or your cover is plain and doesn't stand up against the competition, pay out for someone else to do it. You could write the best book in the world, but if your cover is unattractive and boring, you are going to struggle to make sales.

We'll talk in a minute about how to find cheap, talented designers.

Researching a Quality Cover

When starting out, you may not have an idea of what makes a good cover for a book. It is unlikely you have thought about it much, even when buying books as it is a subconscious decision-making process. We'll talk in a minute about what you can do to influence that sub-conscious process and grab your readers by the eyes.

Firstly though, you need to understand what makes a good cover.

Here you are going to research specifically in your genre or niche. If you write dystopian future books, then it is no good looking at romance covers. If you write self-help books, then the covers will be very different to beauty books. If you book cover does not accurately reflect your niche or genre, then you will struggle to make sales as people will not know instantly what your book is about.

There are two ways of approaching this, and it depends on your preference as to which you choose. One involves leaving the comfort of your computer, and the other involves no movement whatsoever.

The first method, which I find to be very good, is to go into your local bookshop and find the section where your future book would be located. Go through all of the books in that section and look at the covers. Check out the spine, the back and, most importantly, the front.

Look at the type of picture, the colors used, where the title is located, the color of the title, the location of the author's name and so on. See which covers grab your attention and make you want to read more, but also look for the similarities between the books. When you've looked at a few dozen books, you will start to realize that there is a theme. There will be certain components making up the cover image which are consistent, certain positioning of the title, certain font types used and so on.

The advantage of a bookshop is that you are looking at traditionally published books, which means the covers have been approved by a publisher and have been professionally produced. This means you know these are conforming, in the most part, to the required themes of that genre or niche.

Alternatively, you can spend some time on Amazon browsing the top 100 lists (www.amazon.com/bestsellers) in the categories where you would list your book. Look at the covers and see which grab your attention. Look for the similarities between the covers as this will tell you what is working and expected by readers.

This is a great way for you to understand what is expected on the cover in your niche. It is important that you adhere to these themes because readers expect them. Although there are a few books that can get away with going against the grain, most books will follow similar themes for the cover, which the readers want to see.

Take notes as you are doing this because this is information you will need to pass to your cover designer so they can produce something that is going to grab attention and sell your book.

Components of a Best Selling Cover

Now you have an understanding of what is required by your readers for your cover; you need to have an understanding of some of the other key components that you need to consider. Your cover designer should know these already, but you need to ensure that their covers meet these specifications.

Clearly Indicates The Genre
The picture on the cover should clearly indicate the genre, so the reader knows the subject of the book. This is one of the first judgment calls a reader

will make when looking at the cover.

If your book is a romance book, then your reader expects to see a good looking man and woman on the cover. The background image will usually indicate the setting of the book, e.g. A jungle for a jungle book, plains for a Wild West book and so on.

A sci-fi book that has a couple embracing on the cover is unlikely to sell because the majority of people will assume it is a romance book. Your target market will mostly ignore the book while romance readers may buy it and then get upset, leaving negative reviews, when they realize it isn't a romance book!

Make sure that your reader can determine the genre of your book or the subject if nonfiction, from the cover. This is the first step in making sales.

Clear Title
The title needs to be clear and easy to read. Sure, that fancy font looks great, but can you read what the words say? More importantly, when it is shrunk down to thumbnail size, which it is in the Amazon search results, can you still clearly read each of the words.

When you were doing your research on book covers, how many covers did you notice where you couldn't clearly read the title because it used a fancy font? How many titles were clear in thumbnail view.

If you were looking at the top 100 lists, then I'm willing to bet that most of the books had a legible, easy to read the title!

Author Name
Your cover needs to have your author name on it. As an Indie publisher, the author name is of secondary importance. Usually, it is located at the bottom of the cover and in a smaller font than the title. Remember, most people haven't got a clue who you are (no offense intended) and so do not care about your name. You are, at least not yet, not a big enough author to sell books based purely on your name.

Look at Stephen King books as well as books by other bestselling authors, and you will notice something very interesting compared to Indie published books. Their names are usually at the top of the cover and in the largest font.

Why? Purely because people buy the books based on the author. A Stephen King fan will pick up a book and buy it purely because it has the name "Stephen King" emblazoned on the front in large letters! They aren't overly fussed what the book is about, Stephen King writes horror, they like horror. Therefore they will buy the book because it is Stephen King.

Until you are a bestselling author and your name alone can sell books this will not work for you. Until you have a large fan base, your book title needs to be the center of attention on the cover with your name being of secondary importance. This is one reason why an attention grabbing title is also important.

Attention Grabbing

Your cover needs to grab attention. How many of the best-selling books grabbed your attention from the cover alone.

The idea is that your book cover encourages the reader to pick up your book and read the blurb. In Amazon terms, this means click on your book and read more about it.

The covers that get the highest click through rates and the most sales are those that have the best attention grabbing covers.

Make sure your book meets the expectations of your readers and captures their attention as you will see a significant increase in sales purely because of the cover. A poorly selling book can often be resuscitated purely by changing the cover, which gives you an indication of how important this is.

Suitable for Advertising

One of the ways you can make sales is by advertising on Amazon (AMS adverts) or on Facebook. These have strict rules about what they will accept. If your book cover features nudity or even a bare chested man then it can be rejected from the advertising network.

In most genres, the cover is not going to upset any advertisers, but in the case of erotica and romance, you need to think about the cover and how you are going to use it in advertising. This may influence your choice of covers and art work.

Branding Your Cover

If you are planning on writing a series or multiple books on a single subject, then you need to consider branding your covers. This means using a consistent layout, design, font and colors so that when readers see one of your books, they know it is your book and part of the same series.

This can be very helpful when you have a number of books out on a single subject and have started to build a reputation.

I had half a dozen books published on a single subject, and one, in particular, was outselling the rest by about ten to one. Significant huh? Yeah, that's what I thought too.

When I looked at my books, I instantly noticed how that particular book cover jumped out and grabbed attention, which contributed to the increased sales. I'd obviously got something right on the cover, so I quickly redesigned the covers for the rest of the books on that subject to follow the same thing and saw an instant increase in sales from all of them.

I now have many more books on the subject published, and all of the covers are branded so that people instantly know the books are mine. As I am on multiple top 100 lists and have multiple books in a single top 100 list, this makes it very easy for people to identify my books which have led to a significant increase in sales.

I would recommend branding as you are designing your cover if you are planning on building a brand in the niche or around your name. It is better to do it from the start so you are not paying out twice for a cover for the same book. Look at the authors who have multiple bestselling books in your categories and see how their books have been branded.

Looking Good as a Thumbnail

This is one of the key points when designing a cover and one that far too many people ignore or forget about.

When people first see your book in the Amazon listings, they will see a thumbnail size image of your cover. If this does not grab attention, then your readers will never click on the link to experience the glory of your beautiful, full-sized cover.

Tell your designer that it is important that the cover is clear and looks good in thumbnail size. When your cover is delivered, shrink it down to the same size as an Amazon thumbnail to check it out. If you can't clearly read the title or determine the genre from the picture, then you need to get it redesigned.

It is vital that the cover is clear and attention grabbing in thumbnail size.

This is the first contact your potential reader will have with your book, and it HAS to get their attention. Again, I frequently see authors complaining their book isn't making sales but when you look at their cover in the search results, you cannot tell what the book is about. When they've changed the cover, the book starts making sales. Unfortunately, when having a cover, most new authors do not consider this factor, yet it is so very important.

Where to Find Cover Designers

Okay, so now you have a good idea of what you need to put on your cover. Perhaps you have a mental image of it in your head.

What next?

Well, you find a designer, don't you?

But they're not hanging around on street corners or loitering in trendy cafes, though of course, they may be if you can recognize them!

You need to find a good designer and, perhaps most importantly for you, one that you can afford. Sure, you can find a great designer, but once you learn their price you may need to sit down for a little while and have a stiff drink!

A great, experienced, professional designer can cost you anything from $500 upwards. It is not unknown for people to spend $1000 on a single cover. Obviously, when you are starting out that may be a little hard to swallow as it means you've got to sell an awful lot of books before you make a profit.

The cheapest covers will come from new cover designers who are looking to build a portfolio and reputation. These designers will often produce an incredible cover for a fraction of the cost of an experienced designer. If you can find one, then they are well worth hiring, but they can be tricky to find. You are less likely to find new designers in the search engines, but they will be found in Facebook writing groups.

So how can you get a good designer on a budget?

Here are some ideas of the different ways that you can find someone to create your covers for you.

Online Search
Search online for 'book cover designer' and similar terms to find people who

can create your book cover. Look at their portfolio and see if they understand your genre or subject. They may not display prices on their website, but you can contact them for a quote. Be prepared though as experienced designers are not cheap!

Pre-Made Covers

Some designers make pre-made covers and sell these to authors. The advantage of this is that the covers are generally cheaper than having unique covers created. However, the disadvantage is that you have to find one that fits the subject of your book or write a book around the cover!

These are a good way for you to get started with a cheap cover. There are some gorgeous pre-made covers available, and the designer will adjust the cover for you. Often this is just changing the name and title, but they will do other changes, sometimes for a small fee.

Facebook Groups

There are many author groups on Facebook where you will find cover designers hanging out, engaging with their target market. You can ask in an author group for cover designer recommendations, and people will share their designers with you.

This can be a good way to find a new designer who will offer a good deal on a high-quality cover to build a portfolio and reputation.

Fiverr/Gig Sites

These contain some excellent designers that will produce superb covers. Search for 'kindle cover' or something similar, and you will find lots of capable designers who have a portfolio of work.

Look at their feedback and the type of covers they produce. Most of these will typically use one or more stock photos on the cover rather than hand draw a design. However, as you are not paying a lot of money, you can't expect a Rembrandt to be created for you. Some designers produce superb covers, so look through the various designers until you find one you feel can complete the work. Contact them and share your vision for your cover, asking if they can do it. Most are more than happy to talk to you and will discuss your requirements before paying for the gig. Do remember that many of these have English as a second language, so you need to be clear in your communications.

Fiverr is particularly good for nonfiction covers and I get all of mine designed there. A nonfiction cover can be as simple as the book title, a sub-title, then a picture and then your author name. Many designers will, for a fee, give you the PSD file for the design. This is particularly helpful if you are creating a brand as you can then change the title and picture yourself without having to pay for additional covers. Now I have a brand; this is what I do.

You can also find someone on Fiverr who will take your Kindle book cover, no matter who created it and turn it into a CreateSpace cover for you for $5. This is a quick and cheap way for you to get a print ready book cover.

Students
A local college will have art or graphic design students attending it. Contact the college and speak to their teacher as you may find a student who is willing to create you a book cover at a fraction of the cost of an experienced designer. Be prepared to explain exactly what you need and expect, including the dimensions and dots per inch (DPI) resolution required. However, you can often get a very talented young person to create your cover at beer money prices.

CREATING A KILLER TITLE

The book cover is the first point of call in the sales process. It is the key to grabbing a reader's attention. Once your cover has worked its magic, your title needs to draw them in and make them click on the link in the search results. A title needs to tell the reader what is in the book and entice them to find out more.

Therefore, you need to come up with an excellent title for your book. You may not be surprised to hear this is one point many writers struggle with.

How you approach, this is slightly different, depending on whether you write fiction or nonfiction.

With fiction, your title needs to create a sense of mystery and needing to know more, while giving away enough about the book that the reader knows it is for them. This can be quite difficult to fit into a few words, and many authors spend hours wrestling with their title.

With nonfiction, your book title needs to tell people what the book contains and how it will help them solve the problem that has caused them to look for the book in the first place. Typically, the title will tell people what the book is about and then the sub-title tells them how it will help them solve their problem.

Keywords in Titles

There are arguments for and against using keywords that people search for in the titles of your books. For fiction, this doesn't really apply and will negatively impact the quality of the title, but it is important for nonfiction. This section on keywords is purely for the nonfiction authors among you, though it can help fiction authors stuck for ideas.

You can use keywords in the title of your book, but the keywords must not interfere with the readability of the title. Although it is nice to include keywords, you should never do so at the expense of producing a title that appeals to your target market. I've taught for years that search engines don't own credit cards and do not buy products … people do, so your title needs to grab their attention.

Amazon are particularly secretive about how keywords are used on their site, and no one knows how they deal with them. Although some people try to test Amazon to get an understanding, the algorithms are regularly updated and changed to improve the experience for the customer with no notice to anyone. You must remember that Amazon has its focus very firmly on their paying customers and you and I as authors are purely a convenience for them!

I would recommend that you use keywords in your book title as it can help potential customers know that the book is relevant to them. I tend to split the main book title into two parts, the first is the topic, which is usually a keyword and then the second half is a bit more information to help the reader understand the relevance of the book to them. If this second half contains keywords, which it invariably does, then that is a huge bonus!

For example, "Breeding Tortoises – A Complete Guide to Breeding Tortoises At Home" makes for an excellent title. The first two words instantly tell the reader what the book is about and makes for a nice BIG title on your book cover, which will easily be visible in thumbnail view. The reader will know from those two words whether or not the book is relevant to them; then they will read the rest of the title.

The second part of the title also contains the main keyword, and it builds on the first part of the title. The second part tells a reader more about the book, in this case, it is a complete guide and aimed at people who keep tortoises at home. It is also great as additional text on the cover in a font just large enough to be visible in thumbnail view.

Around about this point your reader will, hopefully, decide the book is for them because they want to breed tortoises and they are at home, plus a complete guide will have everything they need to know in it! Now it is up to you to further entice them with the blurb and to deliver the goods, more on that later.

However, we're not yet finished with a title because any good nonfiction book also has a subtitle that gives the reader even more information about the book and why they must buy it!

The Sub-Title
The sub-title is longer than the title, will contain more keywords and build on the information provided in the title, helping the reader to qualify the book meets their needs.

In the above example, a good sub-title may look like this, "Your Guide To Successfully Breeding Rare and Exotic Tortoises That Anyone Can Follow."

Here you are using an important word, 'your'. This gives the potential reader a sense of ownership which can help on a sub-conscious level to make the sale. Another important word is 'successfully.' Obviously, your reader does not want to breed their tortoises unsuccessfully and may have been unsuccessful in the past, hence they are searching for books on the subject.

The 'rare and exotic' part brings in a sense of mystery, encourages the reader to think that maybe they could build a business as a tortoise breeder. Then finally, the last few words reminds the reader that the book is for them because 'anyone can follow' it.

The sub-title is very important in nonfiction, as is the title. You should take some time to build the best titles you can because they will go a long way to helping you may sales. Now, if only there were a way to know what titles grab readers attention.

Researching Titles
Remember you were looking at the top 100 lists of best-selling books in various categories. Well, look at them again and this time pay attention to the titles and the subtitles. Also, search on Amazon using words you would normally use when trying to find information on the subject your book is on and look at the titles of the books on the first page.

Look at how the titles are laid out and what words are being used. If nine out of the top ten books are using 'breeding tortoises' but the bestselling book is using 'how to breed tortoises' then you choose the latter as it is doing something right. Perhaps more people search for the latter term compared to the former? However, if the one using 'how to breed tortoises' is languishing further down than the first position, then you want to use the other keyword.

Analyze the sub-titles of the bestselling books and understand what words and phrases regularly appear.

All of this information is then used to help you craft a title and sub-title. Remember, these are major contributors to your sales process and just by changing the title you can revitalize a dead book. Spend the time at the start of the process getting the title right, and you will make sales faster than if you have to mess around changing the title.

When I have determined a topic for a book, I then decide upon a title and sub-title. These are then sent on to my designer who will create a cover while I do the rest of the process.

Don't rush this step, but don't deliberate over it for days or weeks as you will delay publishing or writing your book. You can change the title later on, but it is a big time saver if you can get it right up front. Once you have published your book, particularly on CreateSpace, changing the title becomes much more difficult, requiring a new edition of the book to be published.

WRITING A BEST-SELLING BOOK DESCRIPTION

The book description is the final component in selling your book. This is where you sell your book by telling potential readers what the book contains, how it can solve their problems or entertain them. Amazon limits you to the number of characters you can use to 4000, so this is a good opportunity to be concise and practice your wordsmithing! It sounds like a lot of characters, but you will very quickly find you run out of words.

With a fiction book, the description builds up a desire to read the book by telling the reader some of what is in the book, while building mystery about the plot and characters. It has to reveal enough about the book to make the reader want to buy it but not give away too much, so they don't have to read the book to find out what happens.

A nonfiction description is more informative and will give away more about what is in the book, without giving away too much. The reader has found your book because they are looking to solve a problem, which the description has to convince them that your book can do.

A good description will tell the reader about the book and then use bullet points to break up the paragraphs and concisely detail some of the content of the book, usually detailing some or all of the chapters. Again, you want to build a bit of mystery to encourage people to read your book such as:

"Tortoise Mating Rituals – Understand everything your tortoise needs to successfully breed with its mate, including the one thing they must have to breed"

This description, although slightly more wordy than normal, illustrates this point. The informed reader may have an idea what the 'one thing they must have' is, but the majority of readers will not. This sentence invokes worry that they are missing out on something vital to making their tortoise breeds that means they need to read the book.

You can't do this in every paragraph as it will annoy the reader, but several of these scattered throughout the description, or blurb as it is often referred to, will help encourage a sense of urgency in your book. You are trying to do something similar with the description for a fiction book.

The last paragraph of your description needs to be a call to action, "Buy this book now to learn how you can successfully breed your tortoises at home and raise their young." You can see this encourages the reader to buy and reminds them of why they wanted to buy the book in the first place, i.e. They wanted to breed their tortoises successfully.

Proof read your description EXTREMELY carefully because this has to be 100% perfect in grammar and spelling. I tend to read it through myself several times before asking someone else to read it for me. Any mistakes here will reflect negatively on your book, which will impact sales. Readers will assume that if you cannot get your description right then, your book is likely to be even worse!

Researching Descriptions

Like you researched titles earlier, you do the same for descriptions. Look at the descriptions for the bestselling books in your niche and see what they mention and how they are phrased. Look at the layout and style used.

This is going to give you an idea of what is working in your niche and what your potential readers want to hear. Use this information to help you write a high-quality description that makes sales, ensuring that you focus on the content of your book.

Back Cover of Printed Books

This description will be used as the basis for the blurb on the back of your printed book. You may need to adjust it and summarize it a bit, but it forms the basis of this description. This will be passed to your designer who is creating your CreateSpace cover.

Formatting Your Description

Amazon provides some limited HTML for use in your description. This can be found by searching online for 'amazon book description html' or clicking here.

This involves using simple HTML tags to change how your book description looks. Use the bullet point tags to make your bullet points look more interesting and the header tags to make your description stand out more. Be careful though that you don't overdo it and that your description still looks good.

The biggest mistake people make when using these tags is to forget to close them, which will make your whole description look peculiar. A tag is closed by repeating the tag but with a / in front of it, e.g. <u> says that everything that follows will be underlined. This is closed with the </u> tag. It is very easy to forget to close the tags, so double check these if you are using them.

Use the formatting to highlight specific words and sections in your description, enhancing the layout. Most people will not use these HTML tags either because they are unaware of them or because they don't understand how to use them. If you use them, then your book will stand out from the crowd because you will have a better looking description, but be careful that you do not overdo it and use too many tags.

A bullet point list is created using the following tags:

```
<ul>
<li>Item 1</li>
<li>Item 2</li>
<li>Item 3</li>
</ul>
```

Add more of the lines with the items on as required. Try to keep your bullet points to a sentence or two at the most. These are meant to be concise and summarize information for your reader rather than overwhelm them with words.

To create a list of numbers rather than bullets you would use <ol> which stands for ordered list.

You can force line breaks by using <br>, which does not need to be closed. To force a new paragraph, you can use the <p> tag, which also does not need to be closed.

A lot of people will shy away from these tags, but use them in your description to brighten it up, emphasize certain points and make it easier to read. This will help you make more sales and make you stand out from many other Indie publishers.

USING PEN NAMES VS YOUR NAME

One of the decisions that you need to make when publishing book is whether to use your real name, a variation on your real name, e.g. Your initials and surname, or a pen name. The latter is where you use a made up name instead of your own.

Before you decide that you couldn't possibly use a pseudonym for your book, realize that there are some very valid reasons for doing so. Stephen King published books under the name Richard Bachman. His reason for a pen name? He didn't want to over saturate the market with Stephen King books and wanted to test whether his books sold on their own merits or because of his name. Funnily enough, when the identity of his pseudonym was revealed, sales of Richard Bachman books went through the roof.

J K Rowling chose to write under her initials because her publishers were concerned that a female author name would deter young boys from reading Harry Potter. Dean Koontz was told, like Stephen King, that authors do not publish more than one book a year so created ten different pen names to publish under because he was writing so much! Ann Rice, a famous vampire author, is actually a pen name. Her real name is Howard Allen Frances O'Brien. However, she also published some erotic romances using the pen name Anne Rampling.

You can see that pen names are perfectly acceptable, so let's look into some of the reasons that you may choose to use a pen name.

To Protect Your Identity
Perhaps you are writing erotic novels and do not want your friends, family, and co-workers to know what you are writing. Maybe you are publishing books while still retaining a day job and do not want your employers to know

you are also working as a writer.

I publish most of my books under my own name, but I have written some books on other subjects which I would rather not have my name associated with. These are published under a pseudonym, so they do not damage my main brand (my name). In certain niches I write in, I use a female pen name purely because the buyers in that market expect to buy from a female and are much less likely to buy a book written by a male author.

To Preserve Your Brand

You may write on a particular subject, like I do, but want to publish in other niches too. If your main niche is self-help and then you publish books on beauty, dieting, recipes, health, pet care and astronomy, you will find that your read through rate will plummet. People who buy self-help are going to want to buy more self-help books. Unless your other books are somehow related to your main topic, it will confuse your readers, and they won't know who you are as an author.

I publish books on two main subjects under my own name. However, I also write on some other subjects too. As these are not related to my main brand, I have published these under another pseudonym. There are about a dozen books all on related topics which are published under one name.

If you are publishing books on a different subject, then look at using a pen name to protect your brand and avoid confusion among your readers.

More Acceptable For Your Target Market

Depending on the subject you are writing about, your target market may have expectations about the author.

For example, how many male romance novelists can you name?

Some markets expect an author to be male or female. Having a name that clearly indicates your sex or, as in the case of J K Rowling, a name which is ambiguous, can help boost your sales. J K Rowling published crime novels under a male pseudonym because that was what was expected by the market.

Tom Huff published romance novels under the pen name Jennifer Wilde. Robert Vaughn published romance novels as Paula Moore, Paula Fairfield, and others.

Yes, it shouldn't be like this in the 21st century, but people have expectations. The books I mentioned previously are all published under a female pseudonym purely because the readers in those niches prefer to see books from a female author. When I did my research, I noticed that all of the best-selling books in those niches were by females, none were by males. Choosing a pen name here has made my books acceptable to the market and helped them climb the bestseller lists.

Collaborations

When collaborating with another author, rather than putting two names on the book cover, which can take up valuable space and potentially confuse the reader, you may choose to use a pen name.

This could be the first name of one author and the surname of the other. Perhaps it will be a made up name.

However, if you are both publishing books under your own names, then you will want to use both of your names on a collaboration unless it is on a completely different subject. Using both of your names helps to build brand recognition and gives you more chance of people buying other books you have written.

The Nancy Drew novels were written by Carolyn Keene, which is not a single person. The books are written by different people, some of whom are men.

Avoiding Confusion

Before you publish your first book, search the Kindle Store on Amazon for your name and see what comes up. If there are authors who have published books either with the same or a very similar name to you, then you may want to use a pen name to differentiate yourself from them.

Using a pen name in this situation will help to avoid brand confusion. If your name is James Smith and someone has published books under that name, then you may want to add your middle name, your middle initial or use a completely different name.

If you are planning on writing multiple books on a subject or the other author has written books on the same subject as you, then a pen name can help you establish a brand identity and make further sales of your books.

You may also choose to use a pen name if your name is difficult to spell. If readers are searching for your name on Amazon and cannot spell it correctly, then they may struggle to find your books. I do know of Indie authors who have used pen names purely so that readers can find them on

Amazon.

Choosing a Pen Name

It can be difficult to come up with a pen name, and you need to think up something that fits with your target market. Don't worry, you aren't going to be creating Facebook profiles and social media accounts for your pen names, but you need to come up with something that hasn't been used by another author, and that sits well with your readers.

Research A Name

Start be researching a name. Look on Amazon and see what sort of names are doing well in your niche or genre. Perhaps initials and surname are doing well, or maybe double barreled surnames perform best.

Jot down a few ideas for names, use baby name websites for ideas for first names if you need to. Then search not only Amazon but also the rest of the Internet for your pen names and see which ones are in use. See if the .com domain name is available too that will give you the best idea of whether or not it is in use.

Avoid using any pen name that could be mistaken for a celebrity as that could potentially end up with you in legal trouble.

You can use a name that belongs to a real person so long as you do not try to impersonate that person in any way and your writing does not negatively impact their lives. It is not identity theft to use someone else's name unless you try to use their name for financial gain.

Claim The Name

Once you have decided upon the best name to use, you need to claim it. The easiest way to do this is to register the .com domain name for it. This gives an indisputable time and date you made your claim to that name. If you want to stay anonymous then pay for WHOIS guard at your domain name registrar. This hides your identity and protects people from working out who registered the domain.

There are many domain name registrars out there, and by far the best is www.namecheap.com. They are very reasonably priced, extremely reliable, and you can often find discount coupons to use with your registration. As a bonus, in many cases, the first year of WHOIS guard is usually free with them.

If you are planning on receiving payments in this name (which if you are publishing purely on Amazon you won't), then you may need to file a Fictitious Business Name Statement, or similar in your country.

Register Copyright

If you want, you can register the copyright. Most people will do this just by publishing a book in that name, but you can register your copyright with the appropriate government agency. Just remember to ensure that the name is kept anonymous using their services if you don't want people to make the connection between you and your pen name.

What Not To Do

Avoid going overboard in creating your pen name. You don't need a back story, a fake photo, a fake photo of your house, car, kids, and partner. You don't need anything other than your name.

Never claim to have any qualifications or credentials that you do not have in real life as you may get prosecuted for fraud. Be careful creating a fake biography as if your readers find out you are not who you said you were they can end up feeling betrayed and angry.

A pen name isn't going to protect you from any legal action against you. Lawyers will be able to obtain your real identity and will do so if required, so do not think that a pen name will allow you to encourage illegal activities.

If you have offered a publisher first refusal or an exclusive read of your manuscript, do not use a pen name to send the same manuscript to another publisher. It will end up getting you into trouble and potentially seeing you blacklisted by the publishing industry.

Determine Your Desired Level Of Secrecy

You may decide to be open about your pen name if asked or you may decide to keep your identity a closely guarded secret. It depends on how it would affect your life if people found out you were writing those books.

If you are writing steamy romance novels but were a Christian minister, or it could affect your marriage, you may want to hide your identity well. If you do not want to jeopardize your day job by your employers finding out you are a writer, then secrecy may be important.

However, if you are just using a pen name to protect brand identity and avoid reader confusion, e.g. You write in multiple genres, then you can be very open about it. Some writers are very open about their pseudonyms and link their web pages together.

Ultimately, it depends on how your life will be affected by your secret identity coming out as to how protective you are about it.

Marketing With A Pen Name
Marketing with a pen name is exactly the same as marketing without one. You would set up social media accounts in that name using an email address created specifically for that name.

As Facebook doesn't like fake accounts, you are best setting up a page on Facebook under your real account or just ignoring Facebook completely if you don't want to compromise your identity.

CREATING A TABLE OF CONTENTS

Fiction books may or may not have a table of contents, whereas in a nonfiction book it is an essential component. Creating it does not have to be a complex and involved process, though it does depend on what tool you are using to create your book.

I write in Microsoft Word. I know there are many other fancy tools out there that you can use which are specifically designed for writers, but for my nonfiction books, Word is perfect. It is easy, I know how to use it, it is cheap (I subscribe to Office 365 and store my files on OneDrive), and it allows me to easily insert pictures, tables, and a table of contents.

With Microsoft Word, you set up Heading styles. Heading 1 is for your main chapter headings. Heading 2 for sub-headings and Heading 3 for sub-sub-headings. I rarely use Heading 3 in my books, preferring bold or italic text instead.

Word will then create your table of contents, using these Headings in the table. It is very easy to do, there's a command to Insert Table of Contents in the menus, and you can choose from a variety of layouts. Then you can simply right-hand click on this and choose to update the whole thing or just page numbers.

This makes life much easier because you are not wading through your book trying to work out where headings are and manually creating the table of contents. For me, it is the easiest solution, though it isn't for everyone.

Other tools may also have methods for creating a table of contents. You need to look through their help or find a tutorial on YouTube to show you how to do it.

Ideally, your table of contents needs to be clickable so that people can easily navigate through your book when reading on an electronic reader. This is automatic in Microsoft Word though may require some extra fiddling in other pieces of software.

A table of contents may seem trivial to you, but in a nonfiction book, it is very important as it gives the reader an insight into your book. Give each chapter a name that gives the reader an idea of what is in that chapter but also encourages them to be excited about reading it.

When they use the Amazon 'Look Inside' feature, they will see the table of contents, and this can give them some extra insight into what your book contains, which can influence their buying decision. With a well laid out table of contents, your reader will understand how your book is going to help them solve their problems and give them the information they want. It can make your book stand out from the competition, who either do not have a table of contents or has a poorly designed one, giving you the edge in sales.

There is very little extra work in creating a table of contents, and it gives your book a better sense of organization, which can make your book look more professional. Any published nonfiction book has a table of contents, and it should be considered an essential component of your book.

CREATING CONTENT FOR YOUR BOOK

This chapter is all about how to get content for your nonfiction book, assuming that you are not already an expert on the subject. When you are writing on a subject that you are not completely familiar with, you will need to research the content to ensure that you provide information that your readers want to see.

Even if you are an expert on your subject, you should still research the niche to understand what your target market wants to know. If you write a book that does not have the information readers are both expecting and wanting, then the book will get negative reviews and will perform poorly. Understanding what your target market wants is vital in producing a bestselling book.

Compare Bestselling Books

The easiest way to find out what people want is to look at the bestselling books in your chosen categories. Look at what they have included in their book by reading through the table of contents. If you consistently see the same information, then this is expected by your target market.

The information you find from this research will form the basis of your book. Write out chapter headings based on your findings. Don't worry about getting a catchy chapter title yet, just write down descriptive headings, and maybe put some bullet points under them detailing what needs to go in the chapter. I tend to create sub-chapter headings for major information and then format the headings in MS Word as Heading1 and Heading2 so I can easily navigate around the book. Word very helpfully has a Navigation pane which displays the headings in your book, allowing you to quickly and easily navigate around your book.

Order these headings so that they flow logically and tell a story. If you are writing about how to build something, you don't jump straight into the building plans; you provide information before that about preparing the site, getting materials, and other preliminary information. The needs to flow in a logical order so that your readers get all of the information they need. However, you should avoid putting supplementary information towards the front of the book, particularly information that some of your readers may already know. Put this towards the end so the novice readers can still find it and the advanced readers do not have to read through pages of what they consider irrelevant information.

Perhaps the reader may not have all of the required knowledge to understand the content of your book or perform the tasks you are describing, so you may include extra information instructing them on these other concepts. For example, back to the building example, you may want to include chapters on how to perform required techniques such as using a hammer or cutting wood at an angle. These would typically go after the main section of the book because they are supplementary information that will be of interest to some of your target market, but not necessarily all of them. You do not want your reader to have to wade through pages and pages of information thinking 'I know this' because they will get bored and likely stop reading your book.

Forums & Facebook Groups

To write a true bestseller, your research should not just stop at the competition. Self-publishing is a fast moving market, and you can easily include the latest information in your book, regularly updating content as it is very easy to republish your book with updates, unlike with traditional publishing. Take advantage of this to keep your book relevant as it will help your book continue to sell. A book that is regularly updated and contains the latest information has a big selling advantage over other books, providing the readers are aware of that!

Search online for forums and Facebook groups that are related to your niche. Spend a few days reviewing these. You are looking for questions people regularly ask about the subject, frequent problems people experience and innovative ideas and techniques relating to your niche.

Incorporate this information into your book, even if you answer common problems in a Tips & Tricks chapter or something similar. Having this information in your book will make it very relevant to your readers. It ensures that you are answering questions that people often have about the subject, which not only helps you appear to be an expert but also makes your book look like a definitive guide on the subject.

I have found that this research helps you understand your target market and the information that they are looking for in purchasing your book. I will often collate the common problems people experience together with the solutions to this problem in a "Common Problems & How To Avoid Them" chapter which is usually just before the Endnote. This chapter goes down well with readers and is used to address any potential questions they may have left after reading the book.

Interviewing Experts

Another good way of researching your book content is to interview experts in your niche or work with them, depending on the subject. You need to ensure that if you are using their material or referencing their work, they are appropriately credited, and you have their written permission. It is always worth mentioning them when talking about information they provided and thanking them in the preface, purely out of courtesy and to foster good relationships with them for the future.

Experts can be found through searching online, visiting Facebook groups and forums and through social media. These experts are often willing to share their information, but you need to be upfront with them that you are researching for your book. They will often help if credited and referenced, but they may not want to share too much if it is going to compete directly with them.

Alternatively, if experts on the subject are out of your reach, e.g. Celebrities or they live too far away, then read their books and websites but do not plagiarize as that will get you in a lot of trouble.

If necessary, look at attending classes on the subject locally or online through sites such as EDX or Coursera which offer university level courses for free. These can be a great source of information on certain subjects and elevate your knowledge quickly.

Experts are a good potential source of information, but you have to use the information they provide your properly and correctly.

All of these sources will help you get the content you need for your book, and then you have to write it out.

Organizing Your Content

The best way I have found to organize your content is to turn the chapter headings that you put together into Heading1 formats. Underneath these, put bullet points for the content you want to use, plus any references to web sites where required. Where necessary, group some of these under subheadings in the Heading2 style.

This allows you to easily move chapters and content around your book to organize it logically. I do not recommend giving chapters numbers because it makes it harder to move them around. By all means give them numbers, if you want, before publishing your book.

Before you start writing any content, move things around until you are happy with the organization. Then you can start writing and reference sections earlier and later in the book as required to make the book flow and sound professional. The idea is that the book flows and 'tells a story' of your subject, leading people from the beginning to the end. Supplementary information goes towards the end of the book so the reader does not have to read through a lot of information that they may already know.

A well-organized book will sell much better than one that is thrown together. Look at some of the competition for your niche, and you will see a big difference between the professionally produced books and the Indie published books. All of the professional books, and the professional Indie books will have a well-organized table of contents and the information will flow well.

For example, if your book is about instruction someone on a task, the logical flow would be step 1, step 2, step 3, step 4, and so on. If you were to organize the book as step 4, step 2, step 1, step 3, then it would make no sense to the reader. When your book structure flows, the reader is more likely to keep reading because they are getting the information they want. This means that they keep the book if they bought it and will be happier with it, plus it means you get more page reads from anyone who has borrowed your book.

It is easy enough to rearrange the order of your book at any time during the writing process. However, the advantage of getting it right when you start means you know what content you have already included and do not end up repeating information which is redundant. You can also easily refer to other content both forwards and backward in the book, and it will make sense to your reader.

Once you have organized your content and are happy with it, then it is time to start writing, which is the easy part!

Private Label Rights Books

Buying private label rights products is possible. These are reports, books or courses that the author is selling full rights to. With private label rights, it means you have the rights to do anything you want with the content, including publishing it and claiming copyright on it. You will also see Master Resale Rights products which differ in that you cannot claim copyright of that product.

Private Label Rights, or PLR, products can be an excellent way for you to get information on your chosen niche. The quality of these varies, with some being excellent, and some not so good.

I regularly use PLR products when writing nonfiction. I never use them as is, and I would strongly recommend you do not. Amazon does not like PLR products being published on their site and will suspend any book that is a PLR product.

Most PLR products are quite well researched and will give you a good overview of the subject. The content is often a little thin, in my opinion, but it gives you a good starting point if you are looking for ideas.

Re-write the PLR content before you use it as a part of your book. Then add extra content to flesh it out. As most PLR reports are usually anywhere from 2,000 to 10,000 words in length, it isn't really enough to be a full-length book. However, it can be a great starting point, giving you some good content to start with.

Search online for your main keyword and the word PLR to find PLR products. You will pay for the PLR rights, but invariably it isn't too expensive. This can be a good starting point for you, but if you are researching your book properly, then there is no need for it. Although I use some PLR from my library of it, I rarely buy it these days, preferring to save my money and spend my time searching online.

When you are starting out, PLR can give you a very good starting point for your new book. Just remember that it must be rewritten and made unique before it is published on Amazon.

Ensuring Your Book is Unique

This is a very important part of being an author, and with the massive increase in people publishing books, it can be easy to infringe on trademarks or inadvertently plagiarize. Less scrupulous authors will either directly steal other people's books or steal content from their websites, which you must never do. This can get you into serious legal trouble as well as get your Amazon account shut down with the loss of all royalties. There is a potential for short term gain, but long term you will not prosper.

As you have written your book yourself, you are unlikely to have to worry about whether or not your content is unique. However, if you are outsourcing your writing, then you may want to run some checks to determine that you are getting a unique book. Although the ghost writer is liable for the breach of copyright, you are the one that will get sued and have to deal with it before making a claim against the writer you hired. You may not be able to track down the ghost writer to pass the blame on to them, or they could be in a country where the legal action has no impact on them.

Therefore, it is important that any content you have written for you is checked. Once you have built a good working relationship with a ghost writer, you will be able to trust them, but certainly, at the start of the working relationship, you will need to double check their content.

Some freelancer sites will run anything you have written through a copyright checker free of charge. These are typically very good as the site has its reputation to maintain and will be more than adequate for your needs.

If no copyright check is run for you, then you need to do your own. This can be done using a paid service, or you can give it a quick check yourself, which is less thorough.

The best plagiarism checker is www.copyscape.com, though you will pay to use the service. However, it is very thorough and provides a detailed copyright check. It can, on occasion, be a bit over-enthusiastic in that it will claim any three or four-word phrase is not unique. However, with a bit of tweaking and common sense, you can get a good idea of whether or not the content is unique.

An alternative method is to take a sentence from each chapter of your book and type it into your favorite search engine enclosed in quotes. Look for a sentence that has something unique or stands out in as that is more likely to give you a good indication of whether your content is okay. This should come back with no results, but if it comes back with any articles or anything else, check it out and see whether other sentences match the content in your book. The odd sentence could be duplicated, but if more content from that page appears in your book, then you have a copyright problem.

In general, I have found ghost writers to be an honest bunch of people. As this is their business and livelihood, it is in their best interests to provide you with unique, genuine content.

What I have found is that there are dishonest ghost writers who provide you with poor quality, duplicate content. These tend to be cheaper writers or more common on article writing sites where they are trying to make a quick buck. When I have seen duplicate content being palmed off on me, it has always been from new writers on a site.

By choosing a writer who is established on a freelancer site with positive reviews or choosing someone who has been recommended to you, you are more likely to get unique, high-quality content. We'll talk more about outsourcing your writing in the next chapter.

It is important that you ensure the content of your book is unique. Amazon takes a dim view of any copyright infringement, and they will stop the sale of your book. In the worst cases, they will suspend your account and insist you provide proof that all your books are unique and that you own the copyright, which is a frustrating task.

A simple check is worth doing and paying for a site like Copyscape is well worth it to protect your investment and ensure your book will be accepted and published.

HIRING GHOST WRITERS & OUTSOURCERS

Some people will outsource their writing, either by hiring a ghost writer or by hiring outsourcers to write articles for them. Before we go any further, let me just say that if you pay peanuts, you get monkeys. Yes, you can hire incredibly cheap ghost writers to write your book for you, but the downside of them is that the book will read dreadfully, be grammatically incorrect and you will spend more time and money correcting it than it would have cost to hire a decent writer in the first place.

Not everyone will hire a ghost writer, but you can hire both fiction and nonfiction writers. If you are not an expert on the subject or you do not have a lot of time, then hiring an outsourcer is a good idea. If you want to produce a high volume of books quickly, then an outsourcer is necessary. Some people want the pleasure of crafting their book and will not outsource any of the writing processes.

I write most of my books myself, but I do outsource some of the research. If I am writing a recipe book, I will hire someone for a few dollars an hour to scour the Internet for recipes that I can use as inspiration. My general plan is that if it is something that I can outsource for a few dollars an hour, I will outsource it. A lot of the research is repetitive and can be done by anyone. It could take me a day to do the research, which is a day I am not writing or marketing my books, so outsourcing this simple work helps me stay focused on what makes money.

I also outsource my cover design. I am, shall we say, less than gifted artistically, so rather than spend hours struggling to produce an amateurish design, I pay someone to produce a professional design. This is commissioned when I start on a book, which means it is completed before I have finished the book, so there is no delay in publishing.

Unlike some authors, I do not outsource my marketing or public relations. I control all of my social media. Perhaps when I am a much better-known author with a significantly larger following I will outsource it, but for now it is more cost efficient for me to do it.

What To Look For In A Ghost Writer

This, I feel, is a tough question. Outsourcing your book content is quite difficult to do because no matter who you hire, they won't be you and they won't have your writing style.

However, if you want to increase your output significantly, then outsourcing is the best way of doing this unless you can manage to clone yourself! Outsourcing works best for nonfiction books, but I have known authors outsource writing fiction books too. Fiction books are often outsourced to university graduates from countries like India where a couple of hundred bucks is a serious amount of money. For anyone writing 'trashy' romance or erotica, this is a good way to crank out a lot of books very quickly.

When outsourcing your writing, you need to give the outsourcer very precise instructions on what you are expecting and want as content in your book. If you have outlined your book as discussed earlier, then you will have a good framework to provide them. They are only as good as the instructions you give them. If you give them poor quality or vague instructions, then they will produce a poor quality, unfocused book. Not all ghost writers will ask for clarification; some will blindly follow the instructions you provide them.

When you do find a good ghostwriter though, you want to treasure them because they are a valuable resource that can make you a lot of money, so look after them and keep them happy!

There are plenty of freelancer sites online or article writing sites where you can find people to produce your content. You can ask your writing buddies for suggestions too or even contact me. As these sites change regularly, I am not going to provide a list here that will quickly go out of date. Search online for terms such as 'hire freelance writer' or 'hire ghost writer, ' and you should find not online some sites full of freelancers but also some individual ghost writer sites.

Before choosing an outsourcer, get them to write a sample piece of content of between 500 and 1000 words. You can pay them article rates for this to be fair, particularly if you are going to use it as content. This builds a good relationship from the start. Get them to write an article for your website, pay them for it and tell them that you are looking for a ghost writer. They'll produce a great article, hopefully, and you get some content for your website. By paying them for this, you are showing them that you will treat them fairly, which means they will be happy to work for you.

Give them a subject to write on, plus a brief outline of what you expect as content plus whether or not you want it written in UK or US English. There are differences between the two which could potentially confuse your target market.

When they have completed this article, read through it and check for grammar, spelling, and content. Make sure it is unique and not copied from the Internet. Once you are happy with the content, then you can ask them to write your book. If you are not happy with the content, then you can ask for corrections to be made. You may feel that the content is just not up to scratch, in which case you won't invite them to write your book. If you feel it is good enough, or with minor tweaks, it can be, then you can invite them to write your book.

Although you can work directly with the freelancer, if you have found them through a freelance marketplace you are best going through that marketplace. That way you have the protection of that marketplace in your dealings with them, and they are going to perform well because they work through that site and need the positive ratings to keep getting business.

Dealing With Ghost Written Content

Depending on how you got your book written you may have a bit more work to do. Some people will get their books written as articles, with each chapter between 1000-2000 words on the subject. These can be written by multiple authors or by the same one. You may have got your book written as a book by a single author.

Whichever you did, you need to read through the content to make sure it is all of a suitable quality, requesting changes for anything that is below par. Once you are happy with the content, I would go through it once to make sure it flows properly as a book. Sometimes the separate chapters will sound a bit jerky when put together as a book, and I have seen comments on books from readers who felt the book sounded like a collection of articles rather than a book.

Outsourcing the writing of your books can be a huge timesaver, but for it to make money, you need to do your research and pick profitable niches. You don't want to be spending $200+ a book only to find it sells a handful of copies a month. I would not recommend outsourcing until you have built a system of choosing niches and promoting your books that works. When you have this process, then you can outsource and see your profits explode. I highly recommend doing the whole process yourself a few times, so you know exactly what you are doing before you start outsourcing.

When done properly, outsourcing the writing of your books can be hugely profitable and is well worth doing. It can help you take your business into five or six figures much quicker than trying to write everything yourself.

THE IMPORTANCE OF PICTURES & COPYRIGHT MATTERS

This section is particularly aimed at nonfiction authors who use pictures in their books. It is extremely important that you pay attention to this chapter because breaching copyright of a photograph could cost you a lot of money through lawsuits and find your books removed from Amazon.

How Pictures Help Your Books Sell

Pictures are an essential component of nonfiction books and help to make sales. Think about most of the nonfiction books you pick up off a shelf – they all have gorgeous colorful pictures in.

Adding pictures helps you to make sales because people expect to see pictures. Most nonfiction books (self-help is an exception) benefits significantly from pictures because it helps the reader see what you are trying to explain to them. Most people learn visually, and a picture is genuinely worth a thousand words. From my research of Indie books, many do not have pictures, and this reflects in critical reviews.

The pictures need to be relevant and of good quality. Crop and edit pictures as required, so they are free from distractions and focus on the subject at hand.

Putting pictures into your Kindle book is easy enough, but adding them to CreateSpace books causes a slight problem. The moment you add color to a printed book, the cost of the book jumps significantly to the point where you would have to charge so much for the book it just isn't competitive anymore!! If you choose the expanded distribution channels, then the cost of the book increases further.

This can be tough because people want color pictures. All of your pictures in printed books need to be 300dpi, otherwise they look fuzzy and blurred when printed.

My approach to this problem is to print all my books in black and white, even those with color photographs in. I then offer every purchaser of a physical book a free copy of the Kindle version which contains the color pictures.

At the start of all of my printed books, I have a message in the middle of the page that says something like, "As the owner of this book you are entitled to a free download of the Kindle version of this book. Due to printing costs, I am unable to cost effectively produce this book for you in color, and so all pictures are produced in black and white. By downloading the free Kindle book, you will receive the latest update of this book and all the full-color pictures."

I then go on to tell them how to download the free Kindle reader. The price matching section of the Kindle setup will allow you to give your book away for free to people who have bought the CreateSpace version.

For me, this is a fair way of ensuring my readers can get a full-color version of my book without me having to price my book so high that it would not be competitive in the market place. My readers seem to appreciate this and sales of physical books are thriving. Only a small amount of people will download the free book anyway, but it is no money lost because they have bought the printed book which has a higher commission attached to it.

I was researching some niches when taking a break from writing this section and found one I was very excited about. I looked at the top four books in the niche and realized they didn't have excellent reviews. On reading the reviews, every single one to three-star review mentioned the lack of pictures. It ranged from the simple 'no pictures' to people stating that they felt the subject was well explained, but some pictures would have made it much easier to understand. Naturally, I will be writing for this niche as just by adding some pictures I can instantly stand out from the competition! I always say that pictures are important and this illustrates their value yet again.

Pictures help your books sell and add a lot of value to your books. Include them in both your Kindle and CreateSpace books, and they will help your books stand out from the crowd of Indie books, helping sales. I have noticed a significant increase in sales from books that have pictures compared to those that do not, so include relevant pictures that add value to the content in your book. Do not include pictures for the sake of including pictures.

Taking Your Own Photos

One option is to take your own photographs and use them in your books. Although you can find royalty free pictures, more on that in a moment, you can struggle to find relevant pictures for some of the more obscure niches. It can also be frustrating to spend hours searching through stock photo sites trying to find just the right picture. Adding pictures to a book is the part I dislike the most about writing, even more so than editing and proof reading! It takes a long time to find the right picture; then you may have to buy it or even put in a copyright notice detailing who owns the copyright if you can get permission to use it. It all becomes a bit of a headache.

Taking your own pictures is often much easier and it helps a lot with the book you are writing. I wrote a cookery book recently and made one recipe from each section and took lots of photos of each step and the finished article. I found this to be useful as I had at least one recipe per section with step by step photos plus I could use the content on my website to advertise the book.

To take your own photos, you need a decent camera. You don't need to spend thousands of dollars on camera equipment, an iPhone or similar camera will do as they take very high-quality photos. I use three devices for my photos. A Sony XZ phone which has a 23MP camera, an iPad Pro and a Panasonic LUMIX LX-100 camera for the more professional shots. Most of my pictures are gardening related as that is my main niche, so I don't like to carry my iPad or expensive camera around so I use my cell phone to take pictures. When I am staging pictures, and I have clean hands, I use the Panasonic camera. I also use this one when indoors as it has a good flash on it plus I have lighting units. I tend to use the iPad less frequently due to the size of it. The main time it gets used is when my cell phone has overheated from being in the sun and refuses to open the camera!

When taking pictures, there are four key things you have to pay particular attention to:

1. Staging
2. Lighting
3. Background
4. Reflections

These are extremely important if you want to produce a good quality picture. Having your own, high-quality pictures makes it much easier for you to include them in your books and saves a lot of time. I obsessively take photos of just about everything and anything related to my niches figuring that one day I might want a picture of it! I keep all my pictures organized in folders on a cloud drive so I can easily find specific photographs when I need them. This has saved me massive amounts of time and money because I have had the pictures I needed for a book to hand.

Staging or Composition

Staging your photograph is very important. Some of mine are pure natural shots with no staging, but then others are carefully staged to look professional. For example, taking pictures of fruits, vegetables or flowers often involves spraying them slightly with water first, so they glisten deliciously. It means thinking about what is in the picture, what shouldn't be in the picture, what needs to be the point of focus and so on.

This is something you will get the hang of fairly quickly, though you can improve your skills by taking a basic photography course. You will learn a lot about composing a picture, which will help you produce great photographs for your books.

Lighting

Another important consideration. If you are taking pictures outside, where is the sun and where are the shadows. You don't want to take photos with your shadow obscuring part of the object of the picture. Is anything casting a shadow on to your picture?

All of these factors need to be considered and is involved in staging your picture so that it looks good.

If you are taking pictures indoors or in low light situations, then you will need decent quality lighting. Depending on the subject and the lighting this could be anything from a ring flash to a photographic lighting set up to an LED panel (ideally with barn doors). This isn't a book about photography, but you have to learn to get the lighting right to produce good quality pictures which your target audience will appreciate.

Background

One thing many people forget is what is in the background of their picture. They are so busy focusing on the main subject they fail to notice what could be lurking in the background.

When taking your own photos to use in a book, you need to pay particular attention to what is in the background of your pictures. You must ensure there is nothing that can identify where you are or where you live, purely from a personal safety point of view. You need to make sure there are no people in the background, no car registration plates or anything else that could identify anyone else. These could cause you problems for using pictures of other people without their permission even if they are in the background!

If your camera is smart enough, set it so that it blurs the background for you, or use a piece of software to blur it slightly. This can help keep attention on the foreground and prevent anything identifiable being seen in the background.

Remove distractions from the background, so the reader focuses on the main subject of the picture. You can either do this at the time or do it later by cropping the picture or using a tool like photoshop to remove background objects.

When I am taking pictures of plants in the garden, I will remove any rubbish, dead parts of plants or other distractions from the background of the picture. I want the background to be as distraction free to keep the reader focused on the subject of my picture.

Pay attention to the background of your picture, and it can reduce your work in processing the picture later on. Depending on what you are photographing, you may benefit from buying either some photographic backgrounds or some single color (black, white, green or blue) backgrounds to take your pictures against.

Reflections
If you are taking pictures of anything shiny or reflective, then be aware of reflections in your photograph. This could be anything from light reflections to reflections of yourself or other identifiable items.

Pay attention to any reflections and angle the photograph so that they are eliminated, and you have a clear photograph of the subject.

Why Copyright Is So Important

Copyright of pictures is a very hot subject online, and it is important that you have the rights to use every picture, from the cover onwards. Photographers are becoming very savvy about the Internet and are now vigorously pursuing infringements on their copyright. Photographs can be worth a lot of money and courts will allow punitive damages to be claimed.

Although you may think you can copy any picture you find online, you cannot. Unless you buy the picture from a stock photography site or find a royalty free picture on another site or take it yourself, the copyright to the picture is owned. Some people will use hacks to download 'free' stock photographs from paid sites, but as these are effectively stolen, you do not have the rights to use them in your creative works. Using them can involve you being sued not only for copyright infringement but also prosecuted for theft!

Many pictures used online contain hidden pixels, watermarks or metadata that identify the original copyright owner. You may well be able to spend the time removing them, but it is far easier for you just to buy the pictures that you need.

Copyright is a series matter. Before you use someone else's picture without permission, think how you would feel if someone took your book and published it online without your permission. You would be losing your income and want the offender to take down the book and pay for the infringement.

Using genuine royalty free photographs that you have permission for means you are building a sustainable long term business. It means you don't have to worry about Amazon closing your account and withholding royalties or being sued. Always use royalty free photographs in your books and on your website to ensure that you are building a legitimate business.

Finding Royalty Free Pictures

There are two options when it comes to finding royalty free pictures online. You can buy them from a stock photography site, or you can find them on a free stock photography site. These both have their pros and cons, as you are about to find out.

Free Stock Photographs

Many of us will start on the free stock photograph sites. One of the best I have found is www.pixabay.com, though there are many others out there.

The advantage of a free site like this is that it is free. You can use the photographs for pretty much anything you want without having to display any copyright notices and do anything you want with them.

The downside of these sites and this is, in my opinion, significant, is that the photographs submitted to these sites tend to be of a poorer quality than paid sites and the selection of pictures is much more limited. I can't verify it, but I do get the impression that many of these pictures are the ones that weren't quite good enough for the paid sites. Although there is a good selection of pictures, you will find the range very limited and that there are more relevant pictures on the paid sites.

Another site you can use is http://commons.wikipedia.org. This is a free site with thousands of photos on, lots of pictures and archive photos too. The search facility on this free site is somewhat limited and finding pictures is a frustrating and time-consuming exercise.

Also, many of the pictures are not royalty free but can be used if you acknowledge the copyright holder and attribute the image to them. This means you are referencing other people in your work, which although I have done in the past, I prefer not to do.

There are two ways you can do this. Firstly, you can put a copyright notice attributing the image to the owner by the image as you use it in your book. Alternatively, you can have a list of pictures in the back of your book and acknowledge the copyright owners there. Either way, works and which you use is entirely up to you and how your book is laid out.

Stock Photography Sites

These are sites where you pay to use royalty free pictures such as www.istockphoto.com, www.depositphotos.com, and many others. The huge advantage of these sites is that you have a wide range of pictures, they are good quality, and you do not have to attribute any copyright.

I personally use depositphotos.com because I find them affordable and have a huge selection of pictures on everything I write about. Also use pixabay.com as well. First I look at pixabay to see if I can find a suitable image and then if I cannot I turn to depositphotos, who offer an affordable monthly subscription that allows you to download one picture a day, with unused credits rolling over to the following months. Any additional photos will cost you just $1 each.

Having the ability to add pictures to your book is absolutely vital if you want to produce a nonfiction book that sells well. Pictures add a lot of value to your books and helps the reader visualize what you are writing about. Readers want to see pictures in nonfiction books, and these are the best ways for you to do that without spending a fortune on photography.

PRICING STRATEGIES THAT SELL

Pricing is, for many people, the toughest part of selling your book. You want people to buy it, but will they pay more than $0.99? What if you price your book at $9.99, will they buy it? It is difficult to get right, and it can cost you sales and income if you get it wrong.

Let's recap on how Amazon pay commissions on Kindle books. Any book that is under $2.99 or above $9.99 has a 35% commission rate, and those books in between these prices have a 70% commission rate. Obviously, this means that the sweet spot for you to maximize your revenue is to price your book between $2.99 and $9.99, but be aware that you are charged a fee for the reader downloading the book, based on the size of the book.

When you get to the pricing section while publishing your book, Amazon does offer an option where it will estimate the best price for you in the niche. This is worth looking at to see how it compares with your research into pricing.

Before you decide on your pricing, research the top selling books in your categories and on your subject. Look at how they are priced. Look briefly at traditionally published books, but not too closely as they are always priced on the higher end of the spectrum as Kindle books, usually close to the price of the physical book. Pay particular attention to Indie published books and look at what price they are selling their book at. Also look at the number of reviews each book has. Write this information down if necessary so you can track it.

What is the average price of books for sale in that niche? How many books are offered for free, and how long are these books? Is their content good or bad? What price are the books with the most positive reviews selling for?

This will give you an idea of the prices that the market will tolerate. If most the books are selling for 99c except for the traditionally published books, then you may struggle to make sales if you price your book higher.

However, please do not think that you have to price your book low. If it is a quality book, which I am sure it is, then price it accordingly and profit from it. Don't feel you have to price your book at 99c because every other ten-page wonder is at that price. Often pricing your book higher will help sales because your readers will perceive it to be a higher quality book because it is more expensive! Yes, people still link price to quality, though we all know that isn't necessarily true.

The pricing strategy I follow is very simple. When I launch my books, they are priced at 99c. This is a good price for people to gamble on your book. If you are an unknown author, then they are happy to try your book as most people won't notice spending 99c. The book will stay at this price, with a couple of free days here and there to boost sales (though free days don't seem to attract more reviews).

Once the book has one 4 or 5-star review that is positive and gives some good information about the book, put the price up to $2.99. Don't be afraid to put the price up. I kept my books at 99c for far too long because I was worried that if I put the price up, no one would buy. Some of these books had nothing but five-star reviews, yet I was frightened my sales would stop if I put the price up.

Eventually, after much persuasion by some author friends, I decided to put the price up on one of my books. It went from 99c to $2.99, so I got the 70% commission rate. Please remember that at this higher commission, Amazon sneakily charges you for delivering the book based on the file size, so please ensure you compress any pictures to keep the file size down – it will massively eat into your profits, as I found out the hard way.

I worked out that on 99c I was making around 35c per book. I figured that by selling the book at $2.99, I would be making around $2 per book, give or take depending on file size. Therefore, selling a single book at $2.99 would make the same amount of money as selling six (yes SIX) books at 99c.

I thought book sales would plummet, but the next day I checked my sales and found that they had stayed the same. Just by putting my price up from 99c to $2.99 for a 45,000-word book with plenty of five-star ratings, I an increased my earnings by a staggering six times! What a pay rise!

Of course, I reviewed the pricing of my other books too. I put up the prices of all my books with positive reviews to $2.99 and re-wrote those that were not selling or had received negative reviews. I also reviewed my CreateSpace pricing strategy and bumped my book prices up to $9.99.

The following month I had my best month ever, sales hadn't slumped but had increased after putting the prices up. In a month where previously I had made about $100, I cleared my first thousand dollar month, earning just over $1200, which was staggering to me.

Now, I am not saying that you should be greedy and I know some people advise you to price your books as high as possible, but you need to be careful. Yes, you can increase the price of your books but be aware that as you increase the price, people have to think about buying it more. If they are not happy with a book, they are unlikely to request a refund if the price is low. The higher the price, the more likely they are to return the book if it doesn't live up to their expectations.

Amazon does provide you a tool that gives you an estimate of the best price to sell your book at, which does work. However, it comes up with some peculiar prices. You must remember we are conditioned to buy at certain price points. People don't like buying at round numbers, such as $3.00 for a book. However, they will happily pay $2.99 for it, saving them a penny but psychologically it is significant because it is cheaper than $3. Why do you think that products in stores are all priced at something ending with 99 or 95 rather than whole numbers? Because those are price points, people expect and are comfortable buying at.

I would recommend setting the price individually on the other marketplaces within the Kindle book setup taking this into account. You can leave it to the default, where Amazon converts $2.99 or $0.99 into the other currencies, but you end up with some really weird prices, which could impact your sales. I go through all of the other currencies and change them to something ending in 99, usually rounding up but sometimes rounding down. Often the Canadian price will be something like $3.08 in which case I will round it down to $2.99, so it is in line with the USA store.

You can increase your price gradually until you get to a point where your sales slow down or stop. At that point, you can determine the best price point by analyzing sales versus refunds together with commission paid. Just remember to have some consistency in your books because if someone buys your book today for $3.99 and tomorrow finds it for $0.99 they are going to be annoyed and could well refund or leave a negative review. Try not to fiddle with the price too often as it can confuse your readers who may hold off buying to wait for a better price.

Pricing your printed book through CreateSpace is done in the same way, though you only have to set the price in Euros (European market), Pounds (UK market) and Dollars (US market). The price you can set will depend on whether your book is in color (which increases the price) and which distribution channels you have chosen. If you are using expanded distribution, which I recommend, then the minimum price you can sell your book at will be higher than if you haven't chosen these channels.

I tend to start my book off at $7.99, which is a good price for a decent length Indie book, though this may be different with fiction. As the book gets more reviews, I increase the price to $9.99. Although I have seen people recommending charging upwards of $15 for your book, you are then competing with traditional publishing books, and I've found sales drop and refunds increase because people expect more than they are getting from the book.

Pricing is a very sensitive issue, and you need to get the price right to make sales. It's about balancing commission with delivery costs and market expectations. The strategy I've outlined above works well for me. I would recommend using that as a starting point for your books and then testing different price points to see what works best in your niche.

Editing & Proof Reading Explained

One of the biggest complaints readers have about self-published books is the quality of the editing and proof reading. Many Indie publishers either don't bother to do this, do it themselves or they hire a cheap proof reader. Having good content is half the struggle in keeping your readers interested, but to avoid negative reviews, which you will get, you need to have virtually perfect grammar and spelling.

Proof reading is where someone reads your book and checks for spelling, formatting and grammar errors. You should always hire a proof reader that is a native speaker of the language you have written in purely because they are more familiar with the language. Non-native speakers can construct sentences incorrectly or in such a way that they appear odd to a native reader, which can cause problems.

Editors come on different levels. A simple editor will read your book, correct errors and ensure the book is consistent throughout. A developmental editor, which will cost more, reads your book, looks for plot inconsistencies and provides advice on how to improve the book. This latter type of editor is most commonly used by fiction writers as they ensure the plot and characters are consistent, providing advice on how to make the book a better read.

Editing does not come cheap and can run into the hundreds, or even thousands of dollars depending on the editor and the length of your book. Proof reading can also be expensive, particularly for longer books. The cost is the main reason many self-published authors forgo hiring people to perform these jobs. Unfortunately, you do get what you pay for, and if you hire a cheap editor, then you are likely to get poor results.

You can find editors and proof readers on any of the freelance sites or ask your author buddies for recommendations. There are numerous Facebook groups full of authors who will be able to point you in the direction of a good quality worker.

With most self-published authors on a budget, these important jobs are often ignored purely because they can't afford it. It adds a significant amount of money to the cost of publishing your book when you add it on top of the cover design and everything else. Particularly as books will usually go through a developmental edit first, then you make the changes before getting another edit or proof read. For fiction authors, in particular, this becomes extremely expensive when you add together a few hundred dollars for the cover and the same again, at least, for the editing. The result is your book has to sell an awful lot of copies before you start to make a profit.

Editing & Proof Reading on a Budget
How can you ensure your book is high quality without it costing you a small fortune?

When you finish your book, walk away for two or three days. Then return to your book and read through it from start to finish. Don't rush as you are reading every single sentence looking for spelling mistakes, grammatical errors and any ways you can improve the content, either by adding more content or reworking existing content. Leaving your book for a few days means you are looking at it with fresh eyes and are more likely to spot mistakes.

Once you have done this, run the spelling and grammar checker in Microsoft Word. Use your judgment as to whether you accept its recommendations; it is not infallible.

Then, if you can, get a friend or family member to read the book, perhaps in exchange for a six pack of beer or box of chocolates. Ask them to highlight any errors, spelling mistakes, grammar errors or anything that isn't clear. When they have finished reading, ask them how they think you can make the book better.

This step is not always possible as you may struggle to get someone to read your book. However, if you can then do it, otherwise there are other things you can do.

Finally, get a subscription to Grammarly, which is an online service that checks grammar and spelling. It isn't cheap, but is much cheaper than hiring an editor! Sign up to their free service but don't pay for anything to start with. Wait a couple of weeks, and they will send you an email offering you a 40% discount, which is when you buy it. Buy the year subscription if you can afford it as when it renews it renews at full price. Therefore, if you get a 40% discount on a subscription for one month, on the second month, you will be paying full price.

Run your book through this service as it will find a lot of errors and help you improve the quality of your book. It isn't as good as an editor, but will certainly help your book be much better. Again, it isn't infallible and tends to remove descriptive words from sentences, which I find irritating, but it does come up with some good ideas and will help you improve the quality of your book.

It is extremely important that your book is well written and reads well. There are grammar police out there who will jump with joy at the opportunity to leave a negative review because of errors in your book. Most people will forgive one or two mistakes, but if there are too many, you can expect negative reviews. Pay particular attention to the first two or three chapters as they are the ones that appear in the Look Inside feature, where your potential reader can see the first few pages of the book. Make sure these are perfect because then people will feel your book is good quality all the way through.

Making sure your book is free from as many spelling and grammar errors as possible will help your book stand out from the self-publishing crowd. You will instantly be head and shoulders above many other writers, which is going to help you make sales and discourage negative reviews. I would recommend that you do the best job you can here and ensure your book is free from errors, it will make a big difference to your readers.

PUBLISHING YOUR BOOK ON KINDLE

The platform of choice for most people is Kindle (http://kdp.amazon.com). This is, as you are probably well aware, a huge marketplace, though there are other outlets for your books, which will be discussed shortly.

Publishing your book here is an absolute must. You will have access to millions of potential customers across the world. Of course, publishing a book by itself isn't enough to make you money as it is unlikely to be found, there is more to do which will be covered in the rest of the book.

The best formats to publish your book in are either Microsoft Word (.doc) or HTML format. These are formats that KDP understands very well and is unlikely to misinterpret and cause formatting errors. However, there are some other formats which can be used which are detailed in full at https://kdp.amazon.com/en_US/help/topic/A2GF0UFHIYG9VQ.

Make sure that your book is well formatted for the Kindle so that it looks good and make full use of the online previewed to ensure the formatting is correct. I use this to check the entire book to make sure nothing is skewed or misaligned.

Before publishing, make sure of the following:

- There is no cover image on the first page – Amazon insert this automatically, and you will end up with two covers on your book which looks odd
- Have a disclaimer/copyright page as your first page or your book title and author name in pure text on the first page
- Have a clickable table of contents as it helps your readers to navigate

through the book

- Check all the headings appear correctly, and the spacing is right around them
- Make sure there are no blank lines at the end of a chapter as this can throw the formatting off
- Ensure all the bullet points, and number lists are correctly aligned
- Check that the formatting is consistent throughout the book – if you are using a space between paragraphs at the start, make sure it is used throughout and you don't change part way through the book
- Have a single space after a full stop. If like me, you naturally put in a double space, simply do a find and replace where you find a double space and replace it with a single space. This will get rid of the double spaces very quickly and easily
- Check all pictures are correctly aligned and do not appear too large. I don't tend to wrap text around them as it can mess up the formatting. If you do want to wrap text then submit your book in HTML format as DOC format can cause alignment issues
- Make sure you have a page, or pages, at the back of your book which includes a list of your other books (providing they are relevant) and information about you, your web page and social media presence
- Request a review of the book if the reader enjoyed it in the conclusion or a separate section at the end of the book

These simple tips are going to help to make sure that your book looks good on your reader's electronic reader, which encourages a positive experience for them. This benefits you because you are less likely to get refunds and negative reviews.

When you publish a new book, you should always publish it as a Kindle book, whether you publish directly through Amazon or via a third party such as Pronoun, Draft2Digital or another service, all of which will be discussed very soon. As the largest book marketplace in the world, you are missing out on a significant proportion of your potential audience if you do not publish here. Personally, I would recommend publishing directly with Amazon for reasons you will understand as you continue to read.

Some people have an issue with Amazon and are not keen publishing with them, yet they are the best marketplace, pay regularly and reliably, they are worth publishing with. So long as you follow their rules, publish a unique, well-written book, then you will not have any issues with Amazon. You only have issues with Amazon when you flout their regulations, such as paying for reviews or trying to game the system. Honest authors do not have any issues with Amazon and can build a solid business based on the back of their hard work. Amazon are the masters of marketing, and when your book starts to perform well, they will start to promote it more and more on your behalf.

Once you have published on Amazon, then you can also publish a paperback.

FORMATTING YOUR BOOK AS A PAPERBACK

A paperback is an absolute essential if you want to be taken seriously as an author. Many people will only publish a Kindle book and will not make an effort to publish their book as a paperback, either because it is too short or they do not want to spend the extra money or time on formatting and an extra cover.

However, what you need to understand is that your reader attaches authority to anyone who has a paperback published. In their heads, it still means traditional publishing, even though you and I know it is self-published. The majority of books that are published as just an electronic version are usually poor quality, short term income generating books that are thin on content. Some readers will judge whether or not to buy a book based on the availability of a paperback copy. I will still look to see if a paperback is available, even if I don't buy it because to me it means the book is better quality. If the author has gone to the effort to format and publish the book as a paperback, then it indicates they have a high level of belief in the book.

Your book needs to be formatted as a paperback. Although KDP helpfully offers to do it for you at the end of the electronic book publication process, the formatting isn't entirely up to scratch, and the book looks peculiar, in my opinion. Amazon may improve this over time, but I prefer to hand format the book to make it look more like a professionally published book. This, I believe, makes a big difference in making sales because people can see a good looking book that looks like it was traditionally published.

Amazon very kindly provides some interior templates for publishing as a paperback, which can be found at

https://forums.createspace.com/en/community/docs/DOC-1323.

This has templates for a wide variety of different book sizes plus there is a version that has content already added and formatted to help you further. I strongly recommend downloading one of these templates and using it. Edit the template and personalize it, but use this as your starting point because it will save you time and effort.

When formatting your book as a paperback, there are some particular points you need to pay attention to, such as:

- Have your title and author name on the first page as indicated by the Amazon templates
- Make sure that sections and chapters start on the right-hand side of the book, inserting blank pages if necessary. Therefore, your table of contents starts on a right-hand page, perhaps with a blank page on the left-hand side, your introduction starts on the right-hand page and so on. With chapters, you can do the same or have them start on the left-hand page, so you don't have large amounts of empty space
- Use the previewer to check the formatting of your book, ensuring all headings, paragraphs, bullet points and number lists are correctly aligned
- Manually copy and paste your content from your Kindle book into the CreateSpace template and use the Microsoft Word format painter to copy the formatting to the copied content. Do this a chapter at a time and format it correctly
- Make sure that new sub-chapters or headings don't start a line or two above the bottom of a page as it looks peculiar, push them on to the next page
- Ensure that your pictures do not push text over a page awkwardly or leave a lot of blank space before or after them
- Shrink the pictures a little compared to the size in the Kindle book, so they do not take up too much space and are too big in your printed book
- If you have any clickable links in your Kindle book that say 'click here' or anything like that, then you need to change them to direct links ... obviously they can't click on your link because it is a printed book!
- Ensure your formatting is consistent throughout the book, i.e. Use of indentation, paragraph spacing, heading styles, etc. This will help your book have a professional feel to it

You can format your book yourself as a paperback, which will take a couple of hours at most. Alternatively, if you want fancier formatting, you can always hire someone to do it for you. There are software tools out there such as www.papeair.com and Vellum (Mac only) that produce very nicely formatted books if you prefer to use those.

Whichever method you choose, format your book separately as a paperback rather than relying on Amazon's automatic formatting. This gives you full control over the formatting and makes sure your book looks professional. It will make a big difference in how your book is perceived and ensure your paperback readers will be happy with what they have bought.

If you don't want to publish through CreateSpace, you can use a service such as Ingram Spark. However, you are charged to list your book, update your book and a yearly fee for keeping the book in their system. Ingram does regularly run offers where you do not pay for listing your book, but you still have to pay anytime you want to make a change.

I will just say that fiction books do not tend to sell as many paperback copies as nonfiction authors do. However, fiction authors should still publish their books as paperbacks because they need the authority that having a paperback gives you. It will help you to stand out from the thousands of Indie publishers who do not and give you two listings on Amazon, which means double the chance of being found by a potential reader!

Another advantage of publishing a paperback is that you can buy copies of it and send them to potential reviewers, newspapers, magazines, YouTubers, and so on as part of your promotions. You can also use them as giveaways to your social media or newsletter subscribers as well as using them for book signings. Again, this will make you stand out from many other publishers and help you to make more sales.

Kindle Paperback vs. CreateSpace Paperback

This is an ongoing project by Amazon and one that will be the subject to a lot of change over the years. I will give you details of what is happening at the moment and how the future is likely to go, but this is going to depend on the direction Amazon takes. However, this will be updated as and when Amazon makes changes, so make sure you download the latest Kindle version of this book to ensure you have the latest information.

For a long time, Amazon has only published printed books on the CreateSpace platform. Recently, they started publishing paperbacks through the KDP platform, with the sales stats of the books appearing together with your sales of your Kindle books.

Over time, Amazon are likely to integrate more and more of the functionality of the CreateSpace platform into the Kindle platform, eventually retiring CreateSpace completely.

Currently, Amazon are running two separate systems, which obviously costs them more money. By integrating them, Amazon will see a significant cost saving plus the author will be able to view all of their statistics in a single place. It means you no longer need to log into two separate sites, but instead can do everything from a single website, which will save you time.

At present, the transition is still underway. Although you can publish a paperback through Kindle, you cannot publish through the expanded distribution channels. Although this isn't going to affect fiction authors, who typically sell very little through these channels, it will have an impact on nonfiction authors.

Kindle paperbacks also have other limitations, in that you cannot order copies at an author's discount price, which you can through CreateSpace. While CreateSpace supports a large number of different size of the book, Kindle supports far fewer and doesn't like non-standard book sizes. Kindle also does not support the ordering of proof copies, which you can do on CreateSpace.

Although these features are not available at the time of writing, they will undoubtedly be introduced over time as Amazon consolidates the two platforms into one. The cost savings of this consolidation will be significant to Amazon and help them to streamline their services and support. How it will impact authors is as of yet unknown, but Amazon will not remove CreateSpace until all of the functionality is moved to the new platform.

My advice would be that you publish fiction books through Kindle and then buy copies for yourself by lowering your list price for the day you are buying, and then putting it back up again. Nonfiction authors and fiction authors who make sales through expanded distribution should continue to use CreateSpace until the expanded distribution is moved into Kindle. If you order a lot of printed copies of your book, then it may benefit you to remain with CreateSpace, but given the cost of postage of these books internationally, this only applies to North American authors. International authors who want to order books are probably going to save money by ordering from their local Amazon site.

There will be a lot of changes here as Amazon continues to develop their services. I will endeavor to update this section as the changes happen but keep an eye on Amazon to ensure you are aware of what is happening and how it affects your business.

SUCCESSFUL LAUNCH STRATEGIES

Launching your book means setting up promotions and developing a strategy to start making sales from day one, i.e. Getting your book found by readers.

Although there are some strategies you can follow, these depend a lot upon your reputation in your market, the number of books you have published, the niche or genre you are publishing in and even the time of year. We'll talk about some different potential strategies here that you can use to launch your book and start making sales very quickly.

Strategy 1 – 99c Pricing
One easy way to start making sales is to price your book initially at 99c. I find this to be a good price where people will take a risk on an unknown author and title. Once you have a few reviews, then increase the price and benefit from increased commissions.

At this price point, your book will appeal to readers who want to know more about the subject, but do not want to pay a lot of money. It's a good way to start making sales and potentially get some reviews. Often people will buy your book because it is cheaper than the competition, particularly when it is professionally presented.

This isn't going to be a fast way of getting your book increasing in the rankings, but it is by far the cheapest method. You will start making sales, but if you want people to find your book, then you will need to do more than just release it at a low price and hope for the best.

Strategy 2 – Free Days

Another cost free method of launching your book is to run two or three free days the day after you have launched the book.

This means that people can download the Kindle version of your book for free and you get no commissions from it. The advantage of this is your book can get a lot of exposure. The downside, quite obviously, is the lack of earnings on your part. The free downloads can help boost your book in the Amazon rankings.

This does work, and you can get anything from a few to a few hundred or thousands of downloads. Unfortunately, what I have noticed is that from these free downloads you are extremely unlikely to get any reviews, which is a big part of what you are after. I have used this method, and in the space of two days I had a few thousand downloads, but no reviews were received.

You can use this method as a way of determining how popular a book is. The more free downloads, the more popular the niche is and the more worth it is spending money advertising your book.

You can use five free days in any ninety day period of enrollment in the Kindle Select program. I have found that in the first day you get lots of downloads, the second day you get fewer and by the third day they have tailed off and are minimal. I would recommend running the free promotion for two or three days at most as it does appear to give your book a boost in the Amazon rankings.

Strategy 3 – Countdown Deal & Social Media Mailing

If you want to maximize your income, then set your price to \$2.99 or higher and run a countdown deal at 99c when you launch the book.

The advantage of this is that you get 70% commission on the 99c rather than the 35% if you had priced the book at that level. Your readers also know that they are getting a discount on the full price, which means they think they are getting a bargain and are more likely to buy.

Combine this with mailings to your social media accounts and newsletter, and you are likely to make a lot more sales because your followers are already interested in what you write and will recognize the deal.

Run the countdown deal for a limited period and then the price will revert to \$2.99. I'd recommend running the deal for three, five or seven days. Choose one and run the deal for that amount of time. The shorter the deal time, then the more urgency is introduced in the offer and the less likely people are to put off buying the book.

As people are paying for the book, you are earning commission, but you are much more likely to get reviews which will help you make more sales. This should push your book up the Amazon rankings, which will also help improve your sales.

Strategy 4 – AMS Ads

This can be combined with the 99c strategy or the countdown deal strategy; it's up to you as you will know your market.

When you launch your book, you set up some AMS ads to run for up to a month to promote the book and get it in front of potential readers. After the ad has run its course, you can determine whether or not it was profitable and worth continuing. More on AMS adverts a bit later on.

This strategy is very effective because people searching for information relating to your niche will keep on seeing your book in their search results, which helps you make sales. The more they see your book, even if on a subconscious level, they will start to recognize your book and feel they know it.

I like this strategy because it boosts sales, you earn commissions, and you are getting good quality sales which are more likely to leave reviews. It does cost you money for the AMS ads, but that isn't a huge amount, as you will learn later.

Strategy 5 – The Nuclear Bomb

This strategy is going to cost you money plus it requires you to be very organized and know when you are going to launch your book, using the pre-order facility. This is going to get your book the most exposure and give it the biggest boost in sales. It should also keep your book selling well afterward as it will have climbed up the Amazon rankings.

In this method, you coordinate your social media promotions, a countdown deal and other book promotions including newsletter swaps. There are lots of sites that will promote your book for a fee, that varies from the reasonable to the extortionate. Some of these book promotion sites are better than others, and it does depend on your genre or niche as to how good the promotions will be. Most of these book promotion sites focus on fiction books more than nonfiction, so if you are writing the latter, you may have to look around for sites that will promote your book.

There are Fiverr gigs where people will promote your book too, which can also be looked at, though make sure they adhere to Amazon's terms of service.

Although there are a lot of different promotions you can run, most people will schedule one or possibly two a day, running a variety of promotions over the first five to seven days. Although you can run all the promotions on the same day, the downside is that you have no way of tracking which promotion was successful and which was not. By running your promotions over several days, you can track which promotions worked well so you can use them again in the future. Remember that many of your potential customers are likely members of more than one of these groups and if they get a promotional message for your book over several days they are more likely to buy.

This type of promotion is very individual, depending on what type of book you have written, so I can only provide you with general guidance here. However, by combining all the different promotional methods, you are maximizing your exposure. Combine this with a countdown deal, and you will make a lot of sales. This initial jump in sales is going to help your Amazon ranking significantly, which means that after the initial promotions have finished, your book will be riding high in the rankings, hopefully on some best-seller lists and still get a lot of exposure.

If you have the money behind you, then this is the best type of promotion to run. However, as many new authors are on a budget, other forms of promotion are more commonly used. By far the best method for anyone on a budget is the social media promotion, which is why it is so important that you build your following on these sites before you have even published your first book.

WHY WRITING A SERIES MAKES MORE MONEY

There are two main schools of thought when it comes to publishing:

1. Write to market
2. Write what you enjoy

The former will make you money as you are writing on subjects that sell. If you are serious about making money online through your writing, then this is a necessity, whether you write fiction or nonfiction.

The latter is often more enjoyable, and in some cases, it overlaps with the first option, and you can make money from it. It many cases though, writing what you enjoy leads to a niche market and potentially limited sales.

Whichever option you choose, you need to maximize your income. Gaining a reader is quite difficult, so you want to maximize your return on investment from every single person that downloads your book. A high-quality book is the first way to do this as they are going to read all of your books, enjoy it, leave a positive review and help you build your business from that.

But there is more you can do.

Publishing multiple books on a single topic is a guaranteed way to make more money. Think about most of the successful fiction books you read. They are very rarely stand alone books and are usually part of a series. People buy the first book, enjoy it (hopefully) and read the other books in the series. They will then look at the other books you have published and may well read some of those if they are based on similar topics. A fantasy author will stick to the broad fantasy genre because they know that their readers will not only read the first series they pick up but are likely to read other books written by them. If the author has a series in fantasy, one in horror and one in sweet romance, their cross-series read through rate will be abysmal because the genres are so different.

The same goes for nonfiction books. Rather than writing a single stand-alone book on a subject, you will write some different books about the subject so that people will not only read the one book but will read the others too. Building a social media following and marketing to them or advertising on Facebook then becomes a lot more profitable because you are not just selling a single book, but the readers that respond to your marketing are likely to read multiple books by you.

For example, if you are writing a vegetarian cookbook you may decide to write other books on a similar theme such as:

- Low-calorie vegetarian recipes
- Vegan recipes
- Gluten free vegetarian recipes
- Tofu recipe book
- Vegetarian meat substitute cookbook
- High protein vegetarian recipes
- High protein vegan recipes
- Vegetarian desserts
- Vegetarian starters
- Vegetarian snacks
- Vegetarian main-courses
- Vegetarian breakfasts

You can see here how out of a single subject we now have a list of thirteen potential books, including the original vegetarian cookbook.

At the back of every one of your books is a list of all your other books with links to them on Amazon. This list is updated every time you publish a new, related book and you republish the book (easier on Kindle rather than CreateSpace). Your reader will read one of your books and then as they have an interest in the subject hopefully buy other books.

You do need to be careful about cross-over content. If your other books have too much of the same content as the original book your reader bought, then they will be unhappy. However, some crossover is perfectly acceptable, just keep it to a minimum – ideally less than ten percent, which keeps you in line with some of Amazon's rules in case you ever decide to give away a book for free.

If you look at successful authors, they will have multiple books on a single subject. If you are struggling to think of ideas for other books on a subject, what about:

- An Introduction To …
- A Beginners Guide To …
- Advanced …
- Applying … To …

You may need to be creative, but there is a lot of possibilities here for you, and if you want to maximize your return on investment, this is the best way forward. You get read through from your advertising, which instantly makes your adverts more profitable because you are not relying on the sales of a single book. You also have more ways of being found on Amazon when a reader searches for information. You also have more potential opportunities to appear in top 100 bestseller lists, which increases your authority and exposure.

As you can see, having multiple books on a single subject will be much more profitable for you. Once you have written all you can on one subject, then move on to a different subject and repeat.

Publishing Regularly
To keep both Amazon and your readers happy, you should publish books regularly. This is more important for fiction authors but still, matters for nonfiction writers.

If you are regularly publishing books, Amazon likes this and appears to give you a bit of a boost in the search rankings, which can give you the edge over your competition. Your readers will be excited to see a new book, and you have more opportunity to talk to your readers over social media and build up interest in the book before it is even published (the pre-sale feature offered by Amazon comes in useful here).

How often you publish is entirely up to you as there is no perfect answer. Some people will claim you should publish a book weekly, which I am not sure how you could do it. Others claim every month, and still others claim every few months. Bestselling authors can publish a book once a year or even once every two or three years, but they have a huge following that are desperate for their books. For the bestselling author, scarcity can help with sales as readers get very excited about the release of a new book, going crazy when it is released.

Publish your books as often as you can. It will depend on your work and family commitments. The more you can publish, the better, but don't let the quality of content slip to a point where you are releasing poor quality books as that will cause more harm than good.

The 30 Day Window

You will hear some authors talking about the mystical 30-day window. This is claimed to help boost your rankings by you publishing a book once a month.

That is an incredibly aggressive publishing schedule which requires a lot of time and organization on your part, particularly with arranging cover designers, proof readers, and editors. However, some authors claim this gives them a real boost on Amazon and helps them make a lot of money. My personal opinion is that it could help you, but how long until you burn out from the pressure?

The difficulty with this is that many new and part-time authors would struggle to publish quality content within this time frame. Although you could publish shorter books, you need to be aware that you may not be able to charge as much so sales can be slower because the books are shorter.

Once you are more experienced, then this could be something to shoot for to see how much it boosts your business, but I wouldn't concern yourself too much with it. Focus instead on producing good quality, relevant books that your readers will love. Create multiple books on a single subject, covering different aspects of the subject without a great deal of crossover and you will find your income increases significantly.

Building an ARC Team

Something else you will hear from other authors is the need for an ARC team. ARC stands for Advance Review Copy and means a bunch of people that get a copy of your book before general release in exchange for a review.

The advantage of building a team like this is that you can quickly gain reviews of your book, which will help sales. The downside is that only around 20% or less of an ARC team will leave a review, meaning you need to give away a hundred or more copies of your book to get a decent number of reviews.

You will commonly find fiction authors with ARC teams as they are not so frequently used by nonfiction writers. However, the principle still applies for nonfiction writers, though it can be harder to build a team of people interested in your niche. With fiction, it is fairly easy to get a group of people together who are interested in Urban Fantasy. It may be harder for you to find a couple of hundred people interested in Matchbox Cars to review your book.

You need to be careful with ARC teams and keep a close eye on Amazon and their rules. At one point ARC teams were acceptable and a part of doing business, but Amazon gets unhappy about what it thinks are reviews that have been gained in exchange for payment. In the case of an ARC team, you are paying them with a free copy of your book. Before you publish your book, you will need to check Amazon's stance on these teams as it changes regularly.

One way people get around Amazon's rules is to publish their book and then offer it for free for a day. During this time the ARC team download it, then they read it and leave reviews. You then start your marketing efforts several weeks later when the reviews have built up. Alternatively, offer the book on a 99c deal and get your ARC team to buy the book at this reduced price and review it.

An ARC team isn't necessary, but it does make the process of getting reviews much easier. However, you have to ensure you remain on the right side of Amazon's every changing rules and regulations as you do not want reviews removed or your account suspended.

You can build an ARC team from your social media following or your newsletter list if you have one. Alternatively, there are gigs on Fiverr which offer to build a team for you. These gigs have worked very well for many authors, and it is worth looking for the different offerings and perhaps building your team that way. It will be easier for a fiction author to build a responsive team compared to a nonfiction author.

Always encourage your ARC team to give you feedback about your book. You are interested in what bits they liked and more specifically in what parts they didn't like and feel can be improved. You can use their feedback to improve your book so that it is better received when it is launched.

We will talk more about reviews a bit later on and offer tips and advice on how to organically grow the number of reviews your book has.

Beta Readers

Beta readers are different to an ARC team. More commonly found being used by fiction writers, a beta reader is someone who reads a pre-publication version of the book. They are not reading to leave a review, though they will often leave one anyway as they are typically a rabid fan of the author. They are reading to look for mistakes and help the author correct them. They will read through looking for inconsistencies, incorrect facts, spelling mistakes, grammar and everything else that detracts from your book.

These are usually built up from people on your social media networks or members of your newsletter. They tend to be your main fans who love having early access to your books. Their help is invaluable and is often used before the final edit of your book.

Whether you build an ARC team or use beta readers is entirely up to you. Not every author does, and it isn't compulsory. Depending on your genre or niche, it may be beneficial to you. It certainly helps with getting reviews, which will help you to boost your sales. I would recommend looking into this and determining whether it will work for the subjects you write about. If it will, then build your teams and use them as it will help you to make more sales and improve the quality of your writing.

REVIEWS – HOW TO GET THEM & WHY THEY MATTER

Reviews are very important for you as an author. Although some writers think they influence a book's rankings in Amazon, which they may do, reviews influence your buyers and are important in making sales.

When you go on to Amazon to buy something you type in some keywords, and then a bunch of products appears. This isn't just for books, but for anything. You look through the products and pick some whose title grabs your attention. At the same time, you are looking at the star rating of the product. If three products appear, one with a one-star rating, one with a three-star rating and one with a four and a half star rating, which are you going to click on first?

The one with the highest star rating. It has been reviewed by buyers who have had a positive experience with it. Therefore you are more likely to buy it because it has social proof that it is a good product. Products with poor reviews are unlikely to be bought unless there is a burning need for it and there are no other similar products, which is unlikely.

I do this all the time, as do most people I know. I've recently bought some electrical items for my business from Amazon. I went through the first couple of pages of search results for each item and read through the reviews of the items that were within my price range. I read the negative reviews of products with high reviews to find out what people thought the bad points of the product was. This led to me discounting some products because there were reports about them breaking easily or they didn't have the functionality I wanted. The reviews influenced my purchases to the extent that I did not buy certain products because of the reviews and bought others due to the content of the reviews.

This applies to books too. As a keen gardener, I regularly buy gardening books, and I always look through the reviews before I make a purchase. The same applies to the fiction I buy, I see a book with a promising title and cover, but the poor reviews it has gained will ensure I don't make the purchase.

Reviews are very important, and Amazon are very protective about their review system. In days gone past you could pay people to leave positive reviews and they would. Amazon, the thousand pound gorilla, has stamped all over this system to ensure fairness of reviews and the integrity of its site. Now, if you are caught paying for reviews, and, please remember Amazon as a collective is much smarter than you or I, then you will have your account shut down and your earnings withheld.

Amazon takes a very dim view of anyone trying to manipulate the system, and as you are relying on them for your income, you need to play the game by their rules. Yes, there are other places you can list your book, but experience says that Amazon is where most of the money is to be made.

You need to gain positive reviews of your book to help it appear higher in the rankings and to boost sales, so how do you get them?

Good Quality Book
Firstly, you need to ensure your book is of the best quality possible. When I started out, I didn't proofread or edit my books properly, and this was reflected in the reviews I gained. The negative reviews put off buyers, and in the end, I unpublished several books, rewrote them, edited them properly and republished them under new titles.

Re-read the section on editing and proof-reading and make sure your book is free from spelling mistakes, with good grammar. This is a very simple step, and it will make sure that you do not give readers an excuse to leave a negative review.

Good Quality Information
The quality of information in the book needs to be relevant to the subject, well researched and interesting. If you have followed the guidelines from earlier in the book about researching your content, then your book will have the information your reader expects and wants.

With a fiction book, you need to ensure the story is engaging and makes sense with all the relevant tropes your reader expects. Sure, some books can buck the trend, but you are inviting trouble unless you are very careful about it.

For nonfiction books, your reader is buying the book to solve a problem. You need to ensure that your book solves that problem and answers their questions. That is going to contribute to obtaining positive reviews.

A Call to Action
Your book needs to ask the reader for a review. Although Amazon will remind your reader to do so, you need to encourage them too. At the start and the end of your book, ask your reader to provide a review. I find asking at both the start and then reminding them at the end after they have finished, helps to increase the number of reviews.

All you need to write at the end of the book is something along the lines of, "If you have enjoyed this book, please leave a review on Amazon. I appreciate your feedback, and it helps me to continue to produce the kind of books you want to read".

At the start, you can write something like, "When you have finished this book, please leave a review on Amazon to give me some feedback and tell me how you enjoyed my book. I read every review and love to hear from my readers."

Feel free to include the link to your book on Amazon, which means uploading your book again after publication. If you have published on other book networks or through a service such as Pronoun or Draft2Digital, then you must not have any references or links to Amazon in your book. You can get around this by uploading a different version to Amazon, or you can just remove the word Amazon from your call to action.

Responding to Negative Reviews

Negative reviews are a part of writing. No matter how hard you try, someone somewhere will decide to give you a negative review. Whether they didn't enjoy something in your book or they are just vindictive, you may never know, but you are going to get them.

Your first negative review is going to be a bit of a kick in the teeth. I know the first time I got a negative review was devastating. I'd poured my heart and soul, or so I had thought, into my book and then someone dares to give me a one-star rating.

Realize that people are going to give you negative reviews and that they are not an attack on you personally. Read through the review and use it as feedback to improve your book.

I eventually got over the negative review once I had gone through the anger and upset of my book being given a measly one star. I then used the review as feedback to improve my book. They criticized the pictures, so I changed them and made them better. They mentioned spelling mistakes, so I properly proof read the book and then I responded to their comment, thanking them for their feedback. I replied to tell them that I had updated the book and that if they contacted Amazon support, they could push out the new version of the book to their Kindle reader.

A few days later the negative review was changed to a positive review with the reader stating that they had had problems and didn't enjoy the book, but the author (me) had responded and updated the book, and now it was great. The temptation to enter into an argument and respond to their feedback negatively was high, but I resisted it and turned the situation around to benefit my business.

Whatever you do, do not get into an argument by responding to the negative review. All this will do is make the situation worse and make you look bad. It will, in the long run, damage your sales and harm your business.

However, there are instances when reviews are given unfairly. I've seen reviews where the reader has made comments about the book which are not relevant or even about that book. I remember one I saw on a fiction book where the reviewer ranted on about the plot and characters and they weren't even in that book! I have even seen reviews where the reviewer has unfairly given away key plot details and twists.

If this is the case and you feel the review is unfair, a personal attack or another author trying to destroy the competition and promote their book (which some do), then report it to Amazon.

Amazon will look at reviews and will remove ones which are not relevant or abusive. However, they will not remove reviews which are critical of your book, so don't go reporting every single negative review.

When your book has multiple reviews, Amazon will list them in the order they feel is best, often with a negative review right at the top, which is the last thing you need. Ideally, you want a positive review to appear first and any negative reviews to appear further down.

There is something you can do about this, but be careful how you approach this. Amazon allows you to say whether or not a review was helpful. At the bottom of each review, it states "Was this review helpful?" You can select yes or no. Reviews that have more yes votes appear first, and those that have no votes appear lower down.

Ask your friends and family to vote the positive reviews as helpful and ignore the negative reviews. Don't get too many people to do this and don't get too many people to do this all at once as it may raise a red flag with Amazon. Ask them to only vote for one review and not all vote for the same one. This can help adjust the order of the reviews so that your positive ones appear first.

Reviews are vital to your business as a writer. Positive reviews are best, but every review should be used as feedback to help you improve your book. If one reader has said they didn't like something, chances are many more agreed but haven't left a review. Only a fraction of readers actually leave reviews, so a single negative review can often reflect the feelings of a large number of people.

Remain professional when responding to reviews and don't be tempted to respond in anger. If the review annoys you, walk away and return to it a few days later when you have calmed sufficiently to respond appropriately. Trying to argue with your readers will alienate them and do more harm than good to your business.

If you have followed the processes detailed in this book, you should be well on your way to receiving positive reviews. These good reviews are going to act as sales people for your book and help you build a solid, sustainable business.

AMAZON RANKING & TOP 100'S

Although we are specifically talking about Amazon in this chapter, other online book retailers have similar systems. We will mainly talk about Amazon purely because it is the one platform you are most likely to use and concentrate on, but the same principles apply to all other retailers.

Every book site ranks the books in some categories based on a wide variety of factors. Choosing the right category is very important because your book won't sell if it is not relevant to what people are typing in as search terms. None of the book sites disclose their ranking criteria. Although some people have performed testing to try and determine these factors, they are regularly changed and varied without notice, so the information gleaned is very quickly out of date.

Ranking well is very important because your book will not be found by prospective readers unless they can find it when they are searching. In an ideal world, your book will be on the first page of results. Your book needs to be, at the very least, in the first few pages. Let's face it, how many times have you gone beyond page three or four when searching for items on Amazon? Rarely. The higher up the search results your book sits, the more sales you are likely to make.

Some people even think the number of people coming to your book page from external sites or search engines also has an impact on book ranking. Whether this does or does not have an effect is unknown, but it could be an influencing factor. It would make sense that this is an indicator used by Amazon in how popular a book is.

Although we do not know what factors influence ranking and how they impact it, we can take some well-educated guesses as to some of what

Amazon, and other companies, look for when placing a book in the rankings.

- Sales – The number of sales your book has made will influence the rankings. It has to. The more a book sells then, the more relevant it has to be to those search terms. You need sales to rank better, but you need to rank better to sell more books … catch 22 isn't it? This is why advertising and social media promotion is so important. It will help you to make sales and give your book a bit of a kick up the rankings. Remember, with millions of books in the rankings it doesn't take more than a few sales for you to jump up the rankings significantly.
- Keywords – The keywords you use when setting up your book will also influence your rankings as Amazon knows your book is relevant to those keywords and will use them to help determine other keywords your book may also be relevant to. Researching your keywords is very important, and they should be used in the title and description but without keyword stuffing. These keywords may also be used by Amazon to help determine additional categories to put your book into.
- Title – The words in your title also probably influence your ranking as they help to tell Amazon what your book is about, which determines what search terms your book will appear for. Use relevant keywords in your title, remembering that your title must appeal to readers as they have the credit card to buy your book.
- Description – Again, your description tells your readers what your book is about, but it also tells the Amazon algorithm how to rank your book. Use your keywords but make sure the description appeals to your readers first and foremost.
- Reviews – The quantity of reviews your book has will likely influence where it sits in the rankings. The thinking behind this will be that the more reviews, the more popular the book, particularly if the book reviews are positive.
- Rating – How many positive reviews your book has and your star rating likely also has an impact on your rating. It would make sense that books that are well received would appear before those that are not.

Exactly how these, and other, factors affect your ranking is not known, but by paying attention to all of these factors, you can give your ranking the best possible chance of being good.

Other factors that are thought to influence your ranking include how frequently you publish books, with some people believing publishing every thirty days or less is best. The quantity of books you have published may also be a factor, as may be having an author central page and keeping that up to date.

Top 100 Lists

Amazon keeps top 100 lists for all of its categories, which are the top 100 bestselling books in each of the categories.

These are great places to get your books into, through sales, because it helps you make further sales. The more top 100 lists you can get your book into, the more sales you will make as people will assume your book is popular, which of course it is, and that you are an authority on the subject, which of course you are.

If you sign up for the book monitoring service at Pronoun.com, which is free, then they will email you whenever your book hits a top 100 list, plus they will send you category suggestions for your book to help improve exposure.

Choosing your categories is very important because you want to appear in these top 100 lists. When you have multiple books published, if your name keeps appearing in the search results then people are more likely to buy because they assume you are an authoritative and established author.

Monitor your presence in these lists and, if necessary, contact Amazon to get them to add your book to other categories, so long as they are relevant to your book. The more top 100 lists you can appear in, then the more books you will sell.

BUILDING A NEWSLETTER – WHY IT MATTERS

Some authors will build up a subscriber base for a newsletter and regularly email their readers, whereas others will concentrate purely on social media. It seems that fiction authors are more likely to build a newsletter base whereas nonfiction authors are less likely to build a newsletter.

The reason for the latter is that many people who buy nonfiction books have a problem that they want a solution for. They are not interested in hearing from the author and may not be a fan of the author. They are more interested in the content of the book rather than the author and their future books. A fiction fan is much more likely to keep in contact with an author because they want to know when the next book is out, find out about other books and so on.

Building a newsletter can be very helpful because when you have released a new book, you can email your list and hopefully make some sales straight away. This will give your book a boost in the rankings and help to kickstart organic sales.

People will feed into your newsletter from three sources:

1.   Social media
2.   Webpage
3.   Books

All of these are used to funnel people into your newsletter, though you can use other services to help build your list.

To build a newsletter, you need three components:

1. A sign-up form for readers to fill in their name and email address which is sent to the …
2. Autoresponder, which is responsible for sending emails and managing subscriptions and delivers an …
3. Incentive to sign-up to your newsletter

That is the basic process for someone signing up your to your list.

You start at the bottom and work your way up when creating your newsletter. Firstly, create an incentive for your reader to give you their email address. This could be an extra report, a free book, a short story. It has to be something of value that your reader will want that is relevant to your book.

Once you have the incentive, you need to create the autoresponder. This is a service that holds the email addresses and is responsible for delivering the emails to your readers, more on this in a moment.

After you have an autoresponder, you need to create a sign-up form. You will direct people from your books and social media to a web page which is a signup form for your newsletter.

Once readers are subscribed to your newsletter, you can either manually send out regular newsletters, or you can automatically send out a series of emails. Which you do depends on some factors which will be discussed shortly. Whatever happens, the first email will contain the incentive your reader signed up for and is sent out automatically. You do not want to have to do this manually as you are significantly increasing the amount of work you have to do, plus your readers may get annoyed waiting for you to send them their free incentive.

Legally you have to include a physical address at the bottom of your emails plus you have to include a method of unsubscribing in every email. If you are not comfortable providing your home address, then rent a mailing address to use. You are breaking the law if you do not do this and an autoresponder service will not allow you to use their services if this information isn't provided.

Managing a Newsletter

How you manage your newsletter is very important. You need to keep your subscribers happy otherwise they will unsubscribe. If they forget they have subscribed because you don't email them very often, then that increases the chances that your emails will be reported as spam and deleted. Spam complaints are taken very seriously, and you can lose your autoresponder account if too many complaints are made.

How often you mail your subscribers depends on some factors. Most people find that once a week is good. It is not so frequently they get annoyed by you clogging up their inbox but is frequent enough your subscribers remember you. Send it on the same day every week and subscribers will get used to hearing from you, hopefully looking forward to reading your newsletter.

Whether you manually write a newsletter every week or queue up emails to be automatically sent again, depends on personal preference and your genre. There is no right or wrong answer; it depends on what works in your niche. In some cases, you will want to share relevant, current information, in which case manually writing your newsletter is best. If you are just sharing information that is not related to current events or time sensitive, then queuing up your newsletters will work well.

People will unsubscribe from your newsletter; it is a fact of life. The number that unsubscribes will tell you how good your newsletters are! If you send out a newsletter and see a big jump in unsubscribes, then you know the content of the newsletter was not well received. Use your autoresponder reporting facility to monitor your unsubscribe rates as well as your open rates, so you know what content is working well in your newsletters.

Managing a newsletter is not difficult, but you need to make sure that it doesn't become a chore to write because otherwise, you will procrastinate about producing it, which then results in you losing your connection with your readers. Don't be too ambitious in the frequency or length of your newsletter, your readers don't want a small book every week, but news, information, and snippets from forthcoming books can help build up anticipation for new releases. Your newsletter subscribers can also be used for market research to find out what your readers want so you can produce more relevant information.

Autoresponder Services

There are lots of different autoresponder services out there from Aweber to GetResponse to Mailrite and MailChimp. The cost varies significantly with some, such as MailChimp, being free so long as you are under a certain number of subscribers.

Which you chose will depend on your needs and budget. Just remember that moving from one autoresponder company to another is almost impossible without losing a lot of your subscribers. Many reputable companies will not allow you to import email addresses, limit the amount you can import or insist readers opt in again to receive your newsletter. All of these result in a significant culling of your mailing list, which you may not want.

There are some factors to consider when choosing an autoresponder, including:

- Deliverability – a newsletter is worthless if it is not delivered to your subscribers. You get what you pay for, and the more expensive autoresponders have a much better deliverability rate than the cheaper or free ones.

- Ease of Use – you don't want to be wrestling with your autoresponder, so take advantage of free trials to have a good look around, set up a newsletter and see how easy it is to use.

- Reporting – quality of reporting is important as it will help you to understand how well your newsletter is doing. Again, take advantage of free trials to look at the reporting facilities of the autoresponder.

- Automation – can you queue up multiple emails to send out automatically over time? Can you send the first email automatically? Can you segment your list or send to specific groups or numbers of subscribers? Depending on your needs, these could be important and helpful.

There is no right or wrong answer when it comes to choosing an autoresponder. Choose one that suits your budget and your needs, remembering that it can be difficult to move subscribers between autoresponders without losing a lot of them.

Although you can host your own autoresponder, I would not recommend it. It is an investment in time, will need regular updating and you are likely to find your deliverability drops to almost zero as your email address gets spoofed, or your autoresponder gets hacked. It is far better to use a professional service, pay a monthly fee and ensure you are getting a reliable, hands-free service.

Components of a Winning Sign-up Form

Many autoresponder services give you a tool to create sign-up forms, or you can create one yourself using HTML. You can always hire someone to design a sign-up form through one of the many gig or freelancer sites.

For your form to work, it needs to attract your reader and persuade them to sign up to your newsletter. For this to work, several components must be addressed:

- Incentive picture – you need a picture of the incentive the reader is getting for signing up to your list. This has to be professional and clear, think of the criteria for a book cover. The idea is that this helps to entice the reader to enter their email address.

- Clear on what is required from the reader – it needs to be very clear to your reader what information they have to enter. Don't try to use strange words to ask for this information, use common terms that people, regardless of their country of origin, can understand.

- Not ask for too much information – you don't need the shoe size and inside leg measurement of your reader. Only ask for information you need. Ask for too much or information that is considered personal, and your sign up rate will drop dramatically. Unless you have a specific requirement, don't ask for anything more than their first name and email address.

- Subscribe button text – this can influence your sign up rate. Rather than the default word, 'subscribe,' try using text such as 'Send me my book' or 'Gimme my freebie' or something that is relevant to your niche or genre.

- Work on all devices – this is very important as you don't know what type of device your reader is using to access your sign-up page. It could be an iPad, a cell phone, a desktop, a laptop or any number of different devices. If your sign-up form doesn't work or display properly, it is going to hit your sign up rate. One of the most common mistakes people make is using Flash code on their form, which means they are instantly alienating anyone who owns an Apple device as Flash does not work on their cell phones, tablets or computers. There are websites online which will allow you to view your website as it appears on different devices. Use one of these to make sure your page looks okay and the subscribe button works.

When all of these have been addressed, you will have a good quality sign-up form that will maximize your sign-up rate. Of course, you can split test different components of your form to try and increase your conversion rate.

Sign-up From Within a Book

Your books must contain a way for your readers to sign up to your email list. Your readers are one of your main targets for sign ups, and as they are reading your book, you may as well convert them into newsletter subscribers.

Include two different methods of signing up, a text link to the page and a graphic which the reader can click on. This makes it very obvious to your reader, and if they struggle to display graphics on whatever device they are reading your book on, they can still see the text link to sign up.

At the start of the book have a page that is dedicated to getting the reader to sign up. The advantage of this at the start of the book is that anyone who uses Amazon's 'Look Inside' feature will not only get to read some of your book, but also see your sign-up form and can sign up to your list. This is why the text link is so useful because they can type the web page address in, if necessary.

As well as at the start, have the same information at the back of the book. Once the reader has finished your book, they could be in the mood for more information. Finding your sign-up form will mean your readers, who hopefully enjoyed your book and want to find out about more books by you, will easily be able to join your newsletter.

Make sure that your book gives your readers the ability to sign up to your newsletter. They are a warm audience, and conversion rates can be decent. You are likely to see a higher sign-up rate from fiction rather than nonfiction, but it is a good way of adding subscribers to your list.

Newsletter Swaps

A good method of promoting your books and of gaining new subscribers is through what is known as newsletter swaps. This is where you mail your newsletter subscribers about someone else's book, and they do the same for you. Typically, writers with similar sized lists will swap mailings. An author with a mailing list of 20,000 is unlikely to want to swap with someone who has a list of just 1,000 subscribers. Swaps are most likely to happen between authors in related niches or genres as there is little point for a horror author to swap with a romance author.

An alternative to newsletter swaps is buying space in someone else's newsletter. Not everyone sells advertising spots in their newsletter, but some people do. These can be a good way for you to reach out to new subscribers and can form a good part of your book promotion strategy.

Once you have built a newsletter of at least a thousand subscribers, you can start looking for swaps while you are continuing to build your list. Look in author groups and approach authors directly to swap mailings.

This is particularly used by fiction authors and can be very useful during a book launch to help boost sales. Most authors are constantly on the lookout for new books they can mail to their list every week in their newsletter so your book can hit the inbox of thousands of potential buyers.

Instafreebie and Similar Services

One way you can build your subscriber base is through a service such as Instafreebie, though there are other services out there that perform a similar function.

This site allows you to create and participate in giveaways. It works best for fiction authors but can work for nonfiction writers too. The idea is you give away something for free, such as the incentive you have created for your newsletter, and in return, people sign up for your list.

This can be a very good way of building your list, but the downside is that you are limited in what autoresponder services you can use as only a couple are integrated into their system.

The other downside of these services is that your new subscribers can often be freebie hunters, i.e. They are not likely to ever spend any money, but are just there for the free books to read. Some will convert to readers and buy, but you can find the number is rather low. However, if you work your list properly and build a good relationship with them, then you can convert them into buyers and the non-buyers can either be removed or will unsubscribe fairly quickly.

Many authors use Instafreebie and fiction authors, in particular, can gain a large number of subscribers in a short period from this service. Just be aware that if you are giving away content from a published book that Amazon does not permit you to give away more than 10% of any book that is enrolled in its KDP Select program. You can give away an extract of your book, but make very sure it is not more than 10% because Amazon will find out and shut down your account.

A newsletter can be a very good way for you to interact with your readers. It can work alongside your social media to ensure you get your message in front of your readers and potential buyers. Used in conjunction with each other, you can interact well with your readers and build a good relationship. This relationship works to your advantage because you can kick start book releases, boosting sales and revitalize books that aren't selling well through emailing your list.

PUBLISHING YOUR BOOK WIDE

Publishing wide is a term you will hear thrown around on author groups. It means removing your book from KDP Select and publishing it on other platforms, such as iTunes, Google Books, Nook, Kobo, and others. Like most topics to do with writing, whether this is beneficial or not is the subject of frequent arguments, and you need to make a decision based on your business and your books. There is no right or wrong answer as it is a personal decision. I'll explain the pros and cons of staying with Amazon versus publishing wide, so you have all the information required to make your decision.

A book enrolled in KDP Select must be exclusive to Amazon, so it cannot be published anywhere else. Doing so runs the risk of having your book(s) removed from Amazon, earnings withheld and your account suspended or shut down. To publish your book wide, you need to remove your book from KDP Select. This can only be done at the end of a 90 day enrollment period. Each time your book is enrolled in KDP Select, it is enrolled for 90 days which automatically continues until you choose to remove your book. You can remove your book from the program at any time, but you must wait until the end of the 90 day period before you can publish your book elsewhere.

When publishing your book wide, you will also need to remove any references to Amazon such as 'leave a review on Amazon', links to Amazon and so on. Remove these and put generic terms in such as 'if you enjoyed this book, please leave a review' rather than stating a site.

Some people love publishing their books wide because it reduces their reliance on Amazon as they can earn money from other publishers. However, other authors feel that the loss in income from their books not being in KDP Select does not outweigh the gain from being published wide.

To help you make the decision, look at your page reads. Over the last 90 days, how much have you made from them? If you do not feel it is a substantial number then perhaps publishing wide could be a good idea. If you are getting millions of page reads, then you are earning a large chunk of your income from KDP Select and going wide may see a significant pay cut.

When publishing a new book, many authors will enroll it in KDP Select for the initial 90 day period to see how well it sells. If it sells well, then keep it in the program, otherwise, take it out, publish it wide and see what that does for your sales. You can always unpublish it later on and return it to KDP Select.

Some people publish their best-selling books exclusively on Amazon with other books being published elsewhere, driving readers to Amazon for the rest of the series. This can work, but you need to keep a close eye on your numbers to ensure you are getting the read through. Plus you need to ensure that you are not giving away anything for free elsewhere that you are charging for on Amazon as it is against their terms of service.

There is no right or wrong answer here. It is a personal decision for each author and for each book they publish. If you are publishing wide, then you are less reliant on Amazon, so if something does happen to your account, you have not lost all of your income. Some people find that publishing wide is better for exposure as their book is in front of more readers. It can increase sales from advertising as people will find your book on the reader of their choice. Though some people prefer to stick with the devil, they know, Amazon, rather than risk going wide.

Make your decision based on your sale figures and what works for you. You can also try 90 days publishing wide and see what it does for your income. If it doesn't meet your expectations, you can put your book back into KDP Select and remove it from the other publishers.

Pronoun

Pronoun is a very useful site which will give you some good information about your books. If you set up a free account and add your books, then it will give you category suggestions, notify you when you get reviews and keep track of your sales ranking, telling you when you are in a top 100 list. This, in itself, is incredibly useful and I would recommend that you set up this free account as this information is very valuable.

Pronoun is part of the Macmillan Publishing Group, which is a major publisher, so it does have solid backing. Through Pronoun you can publish your books to some sites including:

- Google Books
- Amazon
- Apple iBooks
- Barnes & Noble
- Kobo
- Overdrive
- Bibliotheca

New services are added to this list so there may be more available when you read this. The last two services distribute your books to libraries, which can be extremely beneficial in getting your book out to the widest possible audience. You do not have to publish to all of these services and can choose which ones your book is distributed to.

The upside of publishing through Pronoun is that you publish your book in one place, their site, and they push it out to all the other sites for you. They take a commission on the sales and pay you the rest. Sure, this is a pay cut, but you haven't got the hassle of trying to publish to all of these sites. Google Books is no longer taking submissions from individuals and Apple cannot be published to unless you own an Apple Mac computer.

If you are using Pronoun, then I recommend that you do not use them to publish to Amazon. If you use any of these sites for publishing to Amazon, then you are unable to use Amazon Marketing Services (AMS) to advertise your book. This, in my opinion, is extremely limiting so you must publish direct to Amazon and then use a site like this to publish wide.

Many people like Pronoun because of the access to Google Books. Be aware there is a file size limit with Pronoun and many of the other publishers that you could hit if you publish a book with a lot of photographs or illustrations. Check the file size limitations if your book is getting close to 20Mb in size.

Pronoun will convert your book into a .mobi and .epub format which are yours to keep and use how you please. Pronoun uses PayPal to make payments to authors, which some people appreciate, but there are limitations as to which countries can accept PayPal payments. Check their site to see what the current payment rates are, but at the time of writing, it is 70% for iBooks, 50% for Kobo, 52% for Google Play.

Your book will be assigned an ISBN which will list them as your publisher. This has no effect on your business and no impact on the rights to your book.

Pronoun comes very highly recommended and is well worth using to publish your books. It is a relatively easy interface, though reporting is somewhat lacking. However, it is one of the few ways of getting your book published on Google Play.

Smashwords

This site is very similar to Pronoun in that it publishes to a wide range of sites on your behalf. It too will make payments via PayPal, so again, ensure you can create a PayPal account in your country.

Smashwords publishes to a wide variety of sites including:

- Apple iBooks
- Kobo
- Overdrive
- Barnes & Noble
- Gardners
- Odilo
- Bibliotheca

Plus there are many more, with more being added regularly. As well as distributing your book to all of these sites, it will also be for sale directly through the Smashwords store, which gives you another good outlet for it.

One of the big benefits of Smashwords is that it has a wide distribution into libraries and smaller book stores. This can be significant for you if your book is the type that people want to look for in a library. It can be worth using Smashwords purely for the library distribution sites.

One benefit of Smashwords is it allows you to set up pre-orders on iBooks, Kobo and Barnes & Noble, which can help you make sales and boost your book in the sales rankings.

Publishing on Smashwords does not affect the rights to your book. You retain all rights at all times and can remove your books from any services should you wish to.

You are paid 85% of the net royalty from the sale, not from the full book price. This means that if your book is priced at $2.99 you do not earn 85% of that amount, but 85% of the amount Smashwords received for the sale after costs.

One way of using Smashwords is to publish your book on one of the other platforms and use this purely for access to the library market. How valuable the library market will be to you must be tested, but it could be very lucrative when used in conjunction with other book promotion techniques.

Draft2Digital

Like the previous two sites, Draft2Digital allows you to publish your book from one central location to some book distributors for a fee of around 10% of the retail price of the book. Sites you can distribute to include:

- Apple iBooks
- Kobo
- Barnes & Noble
- InkTera
- Scribd
- Tolina
- Playster
- Overdrive
- 24Symbols

There are more in the pipeline, and at the time of writing, they are in negotiation with Ingram, Google Play, and Amazon, so this is definitely one to watch out for.

Draft2Digital does allow you to set up pre-orders, which is a very useful facility used by many authors to build a buzz about new releases.

Unlike other services, D2D is quite flexible in how they pay their authors. You can be paid by PayPal, Payoneer, check or direct deposit. For people in countries where PayPal is difficult to use, this makes Draft2Digital the platform of choice.

They will withhold 30% taxes from your earnings for International users unless you have completed and submitted a W8BEN form to the IRS.

Authors from within the USA will have no tax withheld. This, though, is the same on pretty much all of the sites.

Publishing here does not affect the rights to your books; you retain full ownership and rights. As Draft2Digital assign your books an ISBN they are listed as the publisher, but this has no impact on your book.

Publishing Direct

Although you can use one of the sites detailed above to publish your books wide, you can publish directly to many, if not all of the distribution sites. For most people, submitting a book manually to each site is a lot of effort and for the loss of a small chunk of commission, worth using a service.

One advantage of a service is that it aggregates your commissions and sends you one payment. Many of these sites, when published direct, have a payout threshold. If you fail to meet the threshold, you don't get paid. Most of the sites detailed above have no or a very low payout threshold, and you are more likely to get regular payouts as you don't need to hit individual thresholds.

If you only want to try one or two sites, then it is worth going direct, but otherwise, you may want the ease of using a distribution service. It takes away a lot of the work and gives you more time to concentrate on writing.

Kobo
This is a very popular platform that many authors report making good sales on. They have some excellent marketing tools and resources.

A lot of authors who go wide will publish manually through Kobo rather than use a distribution service because of the marketing tools available. It is worth looking at.

Nook
Owned by Barnes & Noble, this site has a good reputation with many authors. Obviously nowhere near as big as Amazon, it can still be a good site to work with, and they like to build relationships with popular authors.

iTunes
Owned by Apple, this can be a very lucrative marketplace to sell your book in. However, unless you have an Apple Mac Computer, you are unable to publish to this platform. You can use a service such as MacInTheCloud.com, but many authors consider that too expensive and over-complicating a

supposedly simple process.

Publishing on iTunes is one reason people use the distribution services discussed previously.

Google Books
A marketplace that has never particularly taken off and is, at the time of writing, closed to new authors. It is worth having your book here if you can, simply because Google pushes it on Android devices. Unfortunately, if you want to publish through this platform, you will need to use a distribution service.

Publishing wide can be extremely lucrative and is worth looking at if you feel you are not earning enough from your Amazon page reads. It is worth trying your books wide and if you don't feel it is worth it, bring your books back to Amazon, exclusively.

BOOSTING YOUR INCOME WITH AUDIO BOOKS

Once your book is published, selling and has gained some reviews, you can turn it into an audio book. This is a massive market, and people love audio books. Of course, this works better for some types of books that others. Fiction and self-help books are extremely popular as audio books, but cookery books don't work as well.

If your book is suitable for conversion to an audio book, then you should do it. Having an audio book elevates your status as an author even further! Indie authors publish their books as eBooks. Professional authors have a physical copy of their book for sale too, whereas the truly professional, big name authors have audio books too!

In your reader's eyes, you will be a high-level author when you have an audio book, on a level with Stephen King, Anthony Robbins and the big name authors who produce professional audio books.

Want to know a secret? It is really easy to convert your book into an audio book, and it can be done without spending a single penny!

Although there are other sites you can use, ACX.com is very popular to turn your book into an audio version. This is owned by Amazon, and your book will be published on Audible, iTunes and on Amazon itself. This means that when someone views your book, they will be presented with the eBook, the physical book and the audio book, which will make your book stand out as extremely professional.

You have three options when publishing on ACX as to how the audio book is produced.

1. You can create the audio files yourself or hire someone externally to create your audio book and upload the files directly to ACX
2. You can audition for narrators and hire one from ACX, paying them for the production of your audio book. You then retain all rights and all commission
3. You can audition for narrators by paying them on a profit share basis. This means you do not spend any money, but any commission from the sales of your audio books is split 50/50 with them

This latter method is a great way to get an audio book published without having to spend any money.

Publishing your book through ACX is very easy. All you do is create an audition script, which is a chapter of your book and upload your book to the site together with some information about it. Triple check that the title of your book and the author are correct as it can be difficult to correct these if there are any errors. You can provide information to the narrators on what you are looking for, e.g. British accent, American accent, warm tone, professional tone and so on.

Once your audition script is approved, your book is available for narrators to audition for. They will submit a reading of your script for you to listen to. Expect it to take a couple of weeks for you to get a good number of auditions and then you can choose which one you want to use.

When you select a narrator, you enter into a contract with them. They are given a deadline to produce the audio book; then you need to upload the cover graphic (check the requirements as it is different to your book covers) and approve the audio.

You will need to upload the full version of your book for them to produce the audio from. Give it a check to make sure there is nothing in there that wouldn't work in an audio book such as 'click here for more info' and change it to something that does work such as the web address you want them to click on.

Then your book goes through an approval process with Amazon, which can take a couple of weeks. So long as the title on your cover graphic matches the title of your book and the audio is okay, then the book should be approved. The support is very good and responsive as they want to ensure the process is as easy as possible.

Initially, the process will be unfamiliar, just as CreateSpace was the first time you published a physical book, but it is pretty self-explanatory and easy to use.

When your book is live, you can email ACX support and ask for promotional codes for the UK and US stores. They will send you 25 codes for each store that you can use to give away copies of your audio book. You can provide these to reviewers, run competitions for your social media or newsletter subscribers and give them away to friends and family to get reviews and feedback. If you do not email support to ask them, then they will not send these codes. Typically, you will have the codes within 48 hours of asking.

Now your book is live you can promote it through advertising or social media, start making sales and enjoy the benefits of having an audio book.

An audio book adds a lot to how your readers perceive you as a writer, but not all books are suitable for conversion to audio books. It is an easy process for you, providing you are not recording the audio yourself, and you can get started without spending any money at all. The profit share option is a great way to produce an audio book without paying several hundred dollars to a narrator.

If your book works as an audio book, then I strongly recommend that you convert it. It is another stream of income plus it helps build your professional image.

THE IMPORTANCE OF BEING A BRAND

This is a part of being an author that most Indie authors do not understand, but all the successful ones do. When you become an author and start writing books, you become part of the product. People don't just buy into a book, particularly with fiction writing, they buy into an author too.

When marketing your book, you are marketing yourself as well. If you promote your book offline, then you are part of the promotion and brand because people are coming to see you.

It is important you build a brand around yourself. Think of the most popular authors and how they fit into the brand of their books. This is what you are aiming to achieve as it will help you not only sell more books, but also stand out from the crowd of faceless Indie authors. Being a brand is going to elevate your status as an author in the minds of your readers.

There are some things you can do to help you become a brand and stand out from the crowd.

Branding Book Covers

Your book covers need to be a part of your brand. This means that there is some consistency in design, colors, and layout across your books. This helps your reader know that the books are yours, but it builds a brand which will stand out in the eyes of your readers.

Most Indie authors do not brand their book covers, but big name authors do. Therefore, by branding your covers, you are aligning yourself, in the mind of your readers, with big name, traditionally published authors.

About The Author

Every book should have an about the author page at the back of the book. This doesn't have to be pages and pages of information; it can be a paragraph or two. It is just a little bit of information about you, giving the reader a bit of information and directing them to your author website. Yes, you need an author website with a professional domain name, so you look professional.

Even fiction books tend to have a paragraph or two on the About The Author page. It may just say something like "John Smith lives in Montana with his wife, three children, fourteen cats, two dogs and a horse called Gerald. When he isn't writing, he is riding his horse across the trails, pretending he is a Wild West pioneer."

With nonfiction, you can establish your credentials and experience, so the reader knows you are an authority on the subject. This gives the reader the knowledge that you haven't written the book based on a few Internet searches, even though you may have. If you have qualifications and experience in your niche, then include that in your about the author page, e.g. "John Smith has spent twenty-five years working in computing and holds a master's degree in programming. Having written several popular games and apps, he occasionally teaches at his local community college. He regularly runs classes at local schools, helping children learn about programming."

This is a very important page as it will help you to stand out from the crowd and give your books that edge of professionalism.

You can expand this information and use it as an author biography when publishing your books. Again, this is going to provide more information to your reader and make you stand out from the crowd of Indie publishers.

Author Central Page

Your author central page must be set up and populated with information. Link it to your blog, add all your books and add an author biography, based on your about the author info. Remember to regularly update your author central page when you publish new books.

You need to set up an author central page on each of the Amazon sites you use as currently they are not linked. This is annoying, but the author central page is ignored by many Indie authors. Having it set up and populated with information means you have another potential way for your readers to find you. It also means that you can direct people to this page so they can see all of your books, rather than send them to a specific book page.

Search online for "Author Central" by itself to find the Amazon.com page or add the name of the Amazon country you want to find for specific countries.

Using YouTube

YouTube is a great way to help build your brand by regularly publishing videos about your genre or niche. Even if you write fiction, you can still publish a video every week or two about your writing, your universe, your characters and so on.

This is a great way of building a connection with your readers and starts associating yourself with your brand. Remember that the majority of Indie publishers are not going to bother with this, so this is another way to stand out from the crowd. Big name authors are not media shy, so appearing in these videos will help your readers consider you to be a big name author too!

Using a Logo

A logo can be very helpful. Not all authors use them, but they can be a good part of your brand. You can use them on your social media as headers for your pages, as a YouTube header and on your website.

Your logo, though, must be professionally designed and be relevant to your niche or genre. If you are writing sweet romance books, then a logo that looks like it should be in a horror movie is not appropriate.

This doesn't have to be expensive; you can find people online who will design you a very good logo for under $100. Once you have a logo, get it converted into a Facebook page header, a Twitter header and so on. Then you can have consistency in design across your online presence which establishes your brand.

It is important that you establish a brand and that you are central to it. This elevates your status as an author and makes you look more professional.

If you are writing under pseudonyms, then you may want to establish a brand, but you may not want to use a picture of yourself. I'd recommend avoiding using stock photos of a person as your brand. All it takes is for someone to find the photo in use and share it, and it could damage your reputation. In this case, you want to use a logo or other image as the main point in your brand.

CREATING YOUR AUTHOR WEBSITE

An important part of your business is your website. This is a shop window for you and a place where your readers can find out more information about you and your books. Many Indie authors do not bother with a website and so miss out on an opportunity to connect with their readers. I frequently get contacted through my website by readers asking me questions and wanting more information on my books. I know authors who have been contacted through their website for TV and radio interviews, which has done a lot to promote their brand.

A good quality website is vital as it makes you look more professional. All big name authors have their own website, and you need one too if you want to be in the top league.

This is something that needs to be done properly because this is a reflection on you and your business. If your website looks unprofessional, then your readers will assume your books are too and it could harm sales. It can certainly impact any contact from media professionals.

For anyone writing under a pseudonym, setting up a website is a different process. You usually set up a website based on your name, but with a pseudonym, you may either set it up as part of your website or, if you are not revealing your true name, set up another website or no website at all. Be careful not to do anything that can be construed as deceiving your readers as they will be upset if they find up. However, you can set up a website for your pseudonym, include your book information and have no personal information on it.

Choosing a Domain Name

Before you start, you need a domain name. Now you may be tempted by a free web host and end up with a website address along the lines of johnsmith.wordpress.com. This screams unprofessionalism, so you need to register a proper domain name so readers are directed to something like www.johnsmith.com.

This is a professional sounding domain and one your readers will be familiar with from using the Internet. Ideally, you want to use the .com version of your name, but there is a good chance that may not be available so you may need to insert your middle initial or add the word author to the end of your name to find an available domain name you can use.

A domain name will cost you around $10 a year to register a .com, and this is money well worth spending. Avoid the temptation to be cheap here and save money because it will impact how professional you look to your readers.

I recommend using www.namecheap.com to register your domain names. I have used them for years and found them to be very reliable and affordable. You can search online to find discount coupons, and their pricing is very fair. There are no hidden costs, and there are some very good technical reasons to use them (including top level DNS propagation). There are other domain name registrars out there, some making it seem they offer a good deal, but check what you are getting and really paying for, as many of these so called cheap providers end up being much more expensive due to hidden costs.

Once your domain name is registered, set it to auto-renew as that will ensure it doesn't expire, so you don't run the risk of losing your domain because you forgot to renew it.

Choosing A Web Host

As well as your domain name you will need web space, which is where the files that make up your website are hosted. People type your domain name into their browser, which then displays your website. When you choose a web host, you will be given DNS information that you need to put in the correct place in your domain name registration. It's very easy to do, and full instructions are provided by both the web host and the domain name registrar.

It is tempting to choose a free web host such as Wix, Weebly, Wordpress, Blogger and so on, but I would recommend against it. Yes, they aren't going to cost you any money, but they are very limited in what they can do for you. Firstly, you have no ownership of the content. If they decide to shut down your site for whatever reason, and they can do this, then you have lost your content. You cannot get it back and this could seriously impact your business.

Buying web space will cost you under $10 a month, with many web hosts being cheaper if you pay for an entire year all at once. This gives you a lot of flexibility in creating your website and using facilities such as MySQL, mailing lists, unlimited email addresses and many other features offered by a web host. You also have full ownership of your content, and you know it isn't going to get shut down because someone in an office somewhere has decided they don't appreciate your website.

My web host of choice is www.hostgator.com, and I've used them for years. I've found them to be extremely reliable, easy to use and I can run as many websites as I want from the space I have from them. This allows me to not only run my author site but blogs and interest sites in my niches as well without having to spend any more money. There are other web hosts out there, but check what you are getting and how easy they are to use. You can transfer between web hosts, but it can be awkward and involve some down time for your website.

The best option for creating your website is using some free software called Wordpress. I don't endorse free as often it is poor quality, but Wordpress is an enterprise class content management system that is very easy to use and extremely flexible. You don't need any programming experience to use it to create a beautiful website. Hosts like Hostgator provide a method to automatically install Wordpress, and you can buy templates or use one of the many free templates available, including those that are installed with Wordpress.

One of the big advantages of Wordpress is that you can expand the functionality with plugins. These are additional pieces of software that add new features to the core program. They are installed with a click of a button and no technical skills required. You can find plugins to display recent posts, create a contact form, link to Amazon products, add social media buttons to your website and more.

The beauty of Wordpress is that all this is done in a point and click interface with absolutely no programming skills required. So long as you can move a mouse and click, you can create a beautiful looking website. All of mine run on Wordpress and have done for years.

Of course, if you prefer there are other ways to create a website, and you can hire someone to design one for you or use one of the many web designer tools. It is a personal preference, and you need to use what you feel comfortable with.

A professional looking website is very important to you as an author as it is somewhere your readers will go for more information and to keep up to date with what is happening with you. A lot of Indie authors view a website as an unnecessary and unpleasant expense and so try to spend no money at it all. You have to treat writing as a business if you are serious about making money from it, so spend the money on a good quality, professionally hosted website. The cost of your domain name and web hosting is tax deductible as a business expense, so it is offset against your earnings.

This is an important part of your online presence, which is vital to your success as an author. Link it to your social media sites and regularly refer to it from social media. Post new content regularly in the form of articles and other useful information and then post links to this content on your social media accounts. If you are running a newsletter, then have a sign-up form on your website so your readers can join your newsletter.

Using Wordpress you do not need any technical skills to set up a good looking website, but you can hire someone who will create your website for you. Once it is created, regularly add content that is interesting to your readers and relevant to your genre or niche. Having an online presence is one of the key differentiators between Indie and professional authors. Get yours created and make it look fantastic for your readers. Regularly add content and promote the new content on social media to keep your name fresh in the minds of your readers.

USING FACEBOOK AS AN AUTHOR

Facebook is a useful platform for you to connect with your readers. You can set up an author page or even a discussion group so that your readers are not connecting with your personal Facebook page. You want to keep your personal Facebook posts separate from your business at all costs. Keep your business Facebook pages purely focused on business. Do not talk about religion or politics on your page as whatever you post is likely to annoy half your readers. I've heard of some authors claiming they've received negative reviews for posting their political views on business pages. Keep it focused purely on business and nothing else. Of course, if you are writing about religion or politics then your readers will expect to see this on your page, but otherwise steer clear of it.

The big selling point of Facebook is the sheer volume of people who use it, but this is also the biggest drawback of it. The problem is that with so many people using it and so many businesses screaming for attention, it can be very difficult to get your message seen by your readers, even if they have subscribed to your Facebook Page.

Unfortunately, it appears that Facebook wants your advertising dollars and engagement is very low unless you pay to boost your posts. From experience, I find reader engagement to be lower here than on other social media sites. Organically, I get likes and followers far quicker on Instagram and Twitter than I do on Facebook.

However, as an author, you need to have a Facebook page to engage with your readers. They will expect it. Include a link to your Facebook page, as well as your other social media accounts, at the start and end of your book as these are one of the best ways to connect with your readers. You will find that you get much more interaction with your readers through social media when compared to the response to your newsletter.

Your Author Facebook Page

A Facebook page is essential, and this needs to be set up in your author name. If you don't want to use just your name, add the word Author to end of your name so your page name would be JohnSmithAuthor. This helps differentiate between your personal Facebook account and your author page. You may well get friend requests from readers, but it is best to ignore those unless they are your friends. Mixing business and your personal life can often be a recipe for disaster.

You will need header graphics for your Facebook page. These can be created from your logo, picture or anything else you want to use. If you are not comfortable doing it yourself, then find someone to do the job cheaply on Fiverr, which is preferable to taking the time to do it yourself.

Creating a Facebook page is very easy, follow through the instructions on Facebook and add the information you want. You can add your newsletter sign-up form too if you would like.

Facebook does allow you to boost your post, which means it will be shown to more people. This costs money, depending on the demographic you want to target. Results from boosting posts are variable, with some people having good results and other people having very disappointing reader engagement. This is worth testing on a few posts to see what results you get and if it works well in your niche then boost other posts. Results can vary depending on the content of your post.

Once your Facebook page is set up, start posting to it. For best results, you will need to post at least once per day. This maximizes your chances of your message being seen by your readers. Facebook appears to prefer pages which are posted to regularly and your posts will appear more often in people's feeds if you post daily.

Using Facebook Groups

Facebook groups allow for greater interaction with people. They are more like discussion groups whereas a Facebook page purely allows you to post information for readers to view. Their interaction is limited to commenting on your posts; they cannot post to a page.

For fiction authors, a group isn't going to be much of a benefit, but for nonfiction authors, it can be a great way of engaging with your target market.

Facebook groups are very popular with people to discuss their favorite topics. There are groups on pretty much every subject you can think of, and probably quite a few you can't! People talk about their holidays, gardening, hobbies, and interests, with popular groups having hundreds of thousands of members from across the world.

Creating your own Facebook group gives you control over the content and membership of the group. Providing it is fairly moderated and not just used for self-promotion, you can build a good following of readers. As the group grows, you will want to recruit some of the most active members to become moderators, to ensure the group is a harmonious and pleasant place to be. Some groups can quickly degenerate into arguments, insults, and spam, so you need to keep a close eye on the group to keep it under control.

When creating a group, you need to ensure the group has one or more of your keywords in the title. This means that people who are searching on Facebook for those keywords can find your group. There are lots of different options for creating a group, and you need to decide which apply to your group when setting it up. Luckily, there is plenty of advice on Facebook itself that provides a comprehensive explanation of the process.

A group can be very useful for nonfiction authors to encourage discussion within their target market. You can find out their problems, their needs and the information they are after, which you can then use to make your books even better! If the same questions appear time after time, then you know that is a subject that needs addressing either in blog posts or your books.

Facebook Advertising

Facebook offers a paid advertising service that is extremely powerful and can be very effective. Here you will get an overview of the process and how it can benefit you. The actual mechanics of Facebook advertising is beyond the scope of this book, though there is plenty of information available online.

The big draw to Facebook advertising is the targeting. Facebook collects a lot of personal information from its users, from their age to their location to their interests, marital status and more. This demographic information is not available through any other advertising platform, meaning you can target your ads very precisely. Obviously, you can see the benefit of this to your business.

Facebook advertising can be very responsive, but you will need to test adverts on a small budget before increasing the spend once you have a good response rate. When creating adverts, make sure you keep control over the budget. It is very easy to set your advert to run indefinitely with a daily budget and end up with a large, unexpected bill. I would recommend that you set your ads to run for a fixed amount of time on a fixed budget when testing. Once you have refined the advert, then you can increase these figures, though keep a close eye on your response rate to make sure the adverts remain profitable.

Facebooks ads are worth using, they can be very profitable, but they can also be very frustrating. I would recommend researching them thoroughly and testing with a small budget before spending a lot of advertising. Like many other advertising platforms, some authors get good results, and others get poor results.

You can set up adverts to get likes for your Facebook page, to get newsletter signups from your sign-up form or you can direct people to your web site. I wouldn't recommend directing people to any of your books or pages on Amazon as this can be frowned upon by Facebook, but it also makes it hard for you to track your results.

With good testing and tracking, Facebook advertising can be extremely effective. Understand the different types of advert and what you want to achieve. Test the ads before rolling them out with a greater budget, and you will hopefully see a significant return on your investment.

THE IMPORTANCE OF SOCIAL MEDIA

Facebook is probably the best known of the social media sites, but there are plenty more out there. Here we are going to talk about the four big players in the market that, as an author, you need to be involved in. There are many more social media sites, but they can be more niche specific and have fewer users. The sites we will cover shortly have the most users, are best for user engagement and will help you boost your business as an author. However, if your target market hangs out on one of the many other social media sites, then you should be using that to engage with your readers.

Social media has exploded, and the advantage of it is that you can get instant engagement with your readers. I can post a picture on Instagram, and within a few minutes, the likes are coming in from my readers.

Posting on social media multiple times per day gives you the best results because your posts are more likely to be seen by your readers. Like other people's posts too because that too brings your name to their attention and they are more likely to check out your profile.

You can post the same content to all your social media sites, including Facebook. When I post a picture, this is posted to all of the sites detailed below and Facebook to maximize exposure.

The type of content that works well on social media is something that is informative and interesting, without being too self-promoting. The users of social media are not after being sold to, they are after engaging with their hobby, so you have to be subtle in how you promote your books. Your main purpose is to connect with your readers and get your name known in your niche so that when your social media followers are searching for books and see your name, they buy because they feel connected to you.

As an author, you need to use social media. Connecting with your readers is vital to making sales and making repeat sales. When you launch a new book, you can publicize it on your social media and instantly gain sales. If you are looking for a traditional publishing contract, then having a good social media following can be very beneficial to you. Publishing houses want to know what you can do to promote your book, and a good social media following shows you are established in your niche.

Although there are hundreds of social media sites, the following four are the big players that you need to be involved in. These will allow you to connect to your readers and interact with them so they can contact you and you can promote your books.

Make sure that your web site has links to your social media pages so that your readers can easily connect with you there. You will find people prefer to follow you on social media rather than sign up to a newsletter because they have more control over the interaction.

Many of the regular activities on social media can be automated using software tools, most of which require paying for. These will allow you to auto-follow people who follow you, automatically send a message to your new followers, unfollow people who do not follow you, automatically build followers and more. There is a wide variety of tools available, and the features, prices, and availability regularly changes. Search online for these automation tools if you would like to use one to help manage your social media.

One of the most enduring and popular is a service called HootSuite, which has apps for mobile devices. However, there are plenty more out there and some who are focused on specific social media platforms. Before using any automation tool, make sure that it operates within the terms of service of the social media site you are using. Many are considered hacks or black hat and could end up having your site shut down, so you lose your hard earned followers.

Always Use Pictures
All social media sites work best with pictures. Although you can post plain text, you will find your engagement rate increases significantly when you include a picture of some sort. You need to ensure that you have the rights to publish the pictures online, meaning you either use royalty free pictures you are certain you have the rights to or use your own pictures.

Creating pictures with sayings on (memes) encourages engagement and a lot of sharing of your original post. Include your website address on the picture and people will be promoting your business for you! I create a picture meme about once a week in my main niche and always see a significant jump in re-tweets and shares on those days.

From my own testing, I can see that posts with pictures get between five and ten times the attention of a post without. With so many posts on people's feeds, plain text is easy to miss. A picture stands out, grabs attention and instantly tells the reader that the post is relevant to them.

Hashtags Explained

As part of your social media campaigns, you are going to have to become familiar with hashtags and their uses. The easiest way to explain them is that hashtags are keywords. You use a hashtag to indicate the topic a social media post is on. Although you can use them on Facebook, hashtags don't have a huge impact on posts on that site, but Twitter and Instagram rely on them, and you have to use them properly.

A hashtag is indicated by the symbol '#' followed by a word or phrase. You do not use any spaces in a hashtag. Examples of hashtags include #publishing, #publishingbooks, #beinganauthor, and so on. You can see that if you are using a phrase, you simply remove the spaces.

When people are looking for someone to follow or information on social media they typically search on a keyword. These keyword searches are performed on the hashtags used in posts, so if you use the right hashtags, your posts will come up when people are looking for information, and you gain followers. Ideally, your social media account name will include your main keyword.

With Twitter you will have room for one or maybe two hashtags, so make them count! Instagram has a much more generous limit, and each of your Instagram posts should include between three and five relevant hashtags. One major benefit of Instagram is it suggests hashtags when you start typing one in, giving you ideas as well as the number of posts containing that hashtag. I find these extremely helpful when trying to decide which are the best hashtags to use and will always post first on Instagram and then use the hashtags on other social media sites too.

Hashtags are very important, and every post you make should include at least one. They will ensure what you are posting can be found by people and help you to build your followers.

Twitter

Twitter is one of the best known social media platforms, with anyone who is anyone being on it, from the President of the USA to the Queen of England to your favorite superstar. What is good about Twitter is that it encourages significant engagement with people. If you've got a complaint about a company, forget writing to their complaints department or phoning them up. Tweet them … you'll get a rapid response and your problem solved!

It isn't only companies that use Twitter, regular people like you and I, and your potential readers all use Twitter too. By building a presence here, you can engage with your readers and build your reputation as an author and authority in your niche. There is something quite special about tweeting a new release and seeing sales mount up. Plus if you blog regularly on your website, tweet your new blog entries (you can automate this process easily enough) and direct people to your blog.

With Twitter you are limited to a tweet of 140 characters, so you have to think about what you are saying. If you include a link to a website or one of your books, then use a URL shortening service (Amazon provide one when you build an associate link) so that it doesn't use up all of your available characters.

As well as posting your own information to Twitter you can also re-tweet posts from other people. This can be a very good marketing tool if used correctly. Firstly, you can share relevant and important information about your subject with your followers, which they will appreciate. Secondly, when you re-tweet something, the original poster is notified of the re-tweet. This means that they are aware of who you are. Therefore, if you occasionally re-tweet posts from the big names in your marketplace, you will gain their attention, and you can find them retweeting your posts to your advantage. I have used this to get the attention of TV personalities in one of my main niches and get them to re-tweet my posts. In one instance I had an entire Twitter conversation with a TV personality and their followers which helped to establish my authority and saw a significant jump in book sales on that day.

Twitter is an excellent tool to engage with your readers. If you get comments on your posts, always respond to them as soon as you can. Do not leave it too long because the original poster may forget they have posted. It is always best to strike while the iron is hot. I find readers will contact me via Twitter with questions about my books rather than use the contact form on my web site.

Instagram

Instagram is a rising star in social media and is hugely popular. It is now owned by Facebook, having been bought for a cool $2 billion! It is one of the most active and fastest growing social media sites out there and is, in my opinion, far better than Twitter and Facebook for connecting with readers, partly because it isn't swamped by companies yet.

Instagram is all about sharing pictures; you cannot just post text. It provides you with some predefined filters you can use on your pictures to make them look better. In most cases, you won't use them, but I do find that they can help make a picture stand out, particularly the Mayfair filter which brings out the colors in a photograph.

There is a text limit on Instagram, but it is significantly higher than Twitter. You are unlikely to run into it unless you are writing an epic post.

Post to Instagram two to four times a day for maximum engagement and in one of those posts include a link to your book or web site or something similar. The reason being, this encourages people to click on your links and see what you are sharing.

Building your followers is very easy, and people will automatically find you and add you to their Instagram. Every day, spend five minutes scrolling through everyone else's posts and like a few of them. If you see something which you can add value to with a comment, then leave a comment. This increases engagement and helps you get more followers. As with Twitter, you can engage with the big names in your industry which is advantageous for your business.

This social network is highly recommended and is extremely powerful. It is, at the time of writing, the best for authors to engage with their readers and target market. Remember when sharing a book link to state it is free to read on Kindle Unlimited if it is enrolled in the KDP Select program as you will see a big jump in page reads from people checking it out!

LinkedIn

LinkedIn is aimed more at business professionals rather than networking with friends. It is useful for you as an author as you can build a network of publishers, editors, agents, authors, and people who are involved in your chosen subject.

This site is less about sharing cat photos and pictures of your food and more about sharing quality business information. Many corporate professionals are on here, and you can easily connect with experts in your niche. Regularly posting articles and useful information to LinkedIn can help you get noticed by big names in your niche. Many users report connecting with publishers, getting jobs and offers of joint ventures from using LinkedIn.

If you are a nonfiction author, then you should connect with publishing professionals and people who are involved in your main niche. If you are a fiction author, then stick with just publishing professionals. As a fiction author, your interaction with fans will come from other social networks.

Pinterest

This is another site that is generating a lot of interesting and picking up a lot of followers very quickly. Interestingly, it's main demographic is female, with somewhere between 60-80% being female, depending on when the demographic is looked at.

Pinterest is about sharing web content through pinning it on to boards. It's not the easiest of sites to use, but if you are regularly creating web content, then this is a great way to share it with fans. Beauty, health, and recipes are particularly well received on Pinterest, with many writers claiming this is the best way to connect with readers.

You cannot upload pictures directly to Pinterest, which is probably the greatest source of confusion with it. Instead, you have to visit a website, your own or someone else's, and then pin the content on to your Pinterest board.

I would recommend using Pinterest as it is a great way of connecting with readers and sharing content from your website. It has a very active user base and being active here gives you another chance of connecting with people.

As an Indie author, your web presence is extremely important to you. It is going to help you connect with your readers as well as potential readers, which is a very good thing. If you want to gain a traditional publishing contract, then a good social media following will be a very big selling point for you. It is one of the factors a traditional publisher will look at when deciding to take on a new writer.

HOW TO BLOG & WHY IT MATTERS

Blogging is very important to you as a writer for some reasons. Having a regularly updated web page will help your readers understand you are an active author and a real person. They can find out more information about you and your niche(s) and discover information about your books.

The content from your website will also appear in the search engines, so there is a chance that when someone is searching for information, they will come across your site and your books. This can be an excellent source of traffic for your books, plus it helps to establish your authority. I also know writers who have been picked up for TV and radio interviews based on the content on their website, so it can help you from a publicity perspective.

Blogging doesn't have to be hard work. Once you've got your website set up, it is just a matter of adding new content. This needs to be well written, professional, informative and interesting, which sounds like a tall order, but as an author, it will be a breeze for you! Add content once a week, as a minimum. If you can add content more frequently, then do so, but once a week is an absolute minimum for best results in the search engines.

When you add new content, you share it on your social media, which reminds your followers who you are, shows you are more than just someone who shares pictures, and generates interest in your books. Include pictures in your posts, either your own or stock photos. These add value to the post, but the pictures also appear as an entry in the search engines, meaning more chance for your books to be found.

Each article you add to your website needs to be a minimum of 500 to 1000 words long, though if you can write more, then please do so. For longer articles, you may want to consider breaking them into two or more parts so that people stay longer on your website and scroll from page to page. The trouble with articles that are too long is that the reader gets bored and can't be bothered reading it all. If you split the article between multiple pages, then your reader will read the first page and move on to the next if they are interested. The good thing about this is that the search engines monitor how long people spend on your site and how many pages they read while there, so this can boost your rankings.

PLR Rights Articles

You will see something called PLR or Private Label Rights articles for sale. These are articles that someone else has written and is selling for other people to have full rights to use as they deem fit.

The quality of PLR articles vary from the superb to the downright dreadful, so caveat emptor or buyer beware.

PLR can be a useful source of inspiration for articles if you are struggling to think of content to add to your site. However, I would strongly, and imagine that word in a 92 point brightly colored flashing font, recommend you DO NOT use PLR articles as is on your website.

PLR articles tend to get spammed all over the Internet, being used on hundreds or even thousands of sites. It gets to the stage where everyone in your niche has these articles. Unfortunately, Google and the other search engines penalize sites that use duplicate content, i.e. Copy content that is used elsewhere. Curating content, for those in the know, is not the same as duplicate content.

As these PLR articles appear on so many different sites, many of which are spam sites, this content will be penalized by the search engines.

The best way to use PLR articles is to use them for ideas. By all means, buy them, but rewrite the article completely, add some extra content from your own experience. I regularly use PLR content, but as a framework to which I add more information. I would never use any PLR content as it stands without rewriting it. If you don't want to rewrite it yourself, then you can hire people to rewrite your articles at sites such as www.iwriter.com or www.textbroker.com.

Finding Content Ideas

The hard part for some writers is coming up with ideas for articles for their blog. My best advice here is to go check out Google News and see what the top stories are in your niche.

When you write about current, trending topics, there is a good chance your website will catch the wave of this trend, particularly if you share your content on social media. I've known many people who have added content relating to a trending story and found their website visited by thousands of interested people.

As well as looking through the news sites for information, check out your competition. What are they writing about? Think about the time of year, what advice can you give people in your niche for this time of year? Are there new products being released or events occurring that you can write about?

Writing good quality articles for your website is going to help you a lot to connect with your readers. It will also be very good in getting your website found in the search engines. Websites which regularly add content will rank much better than those that do not. Gaining organic traffic through your website can help you make sales, gain media opportunities and build a reputation as an authority in your niche.

Aim to add fresh content to your website at least once a week. Remember that fresh content includes books you have published, videos you have produced and information about pictures you have taken. This helps establish you as an authority and will give you a lot more credibility if you choose to approach a traditional publisher in the future.

BOOKBUB & BOOK PROMOTION SITES

You will hear writers talking about Bookbub in hushed tones, discussing this legendary service that kicks writers into the big time and makes thousands of sales. I'd like to spend a few minutes explaining what this site is, how it works and how it can benefit you as a writer.

The website is www.bookbub.com, which promotes books in a wide variety of niches. Its primary focus is fiction books, but it does some promotions for nonfiction. For the latter, it is not particularly well targeted beyond the category 'nonfiction,' but I have seen numerous nonfiction books promoted through Bookbub.

The site will promote books, for a fee, to interested readers. This can result in thousands of sales, depending on the genre and the book being promoted. The book being promoted is discounted before the promotion, usually to $0.99, depending on the original price of the book. This is best done on a countdown deal, so you still get 70% commission and needs to be in place before the promotion goes live.

Some people will promote their book as a free book. This will see a massive increase in downloads as everyone loves a freebie. However, this isn't going to benefit you unless you are promoting the first book in the series. What you are counting on when promoting a book for free is that readers will enjoy the first book and then buy your second book and others in the series. For fiction authors with a series and a good read through rate, this is a fantastic way to gain massive exposure.

You may think that these deals are just for Indie authors, but I have seen some big name authors promoting their books through this service to revitalize interest and get in front of new readers. There have been some very good books promoted through Bookbub, and I know that many people experience excellent results, though not all do.

Gaining a Bookbub promotion is somewhat of a mythical thing, it is notoriously difficult to obtain as they have fairly strict criteria. However, a well-written book with plenty of positive reviews will be more likely to be accepted for a deal than a newly published book. Be aware that you pay for a promotion on Bookbub and it isn't cheap, but you can get your message in front of tens of thousands of potential readers, making it very valuable. The cost, particularly for the more popular genres, is very high, but it reflects that this is considered the best book promotion available.

Many writers will state that Bookbub has made them a small fortune, but others are frustrated by the lack of results. Nothing is guaranteed with a Bookbub promotion, but a well-written book that is in the right genre will have more of a chance of doing well than one which is not in the right genre. If your book is selling well on Amazon and has some positive reviews, then it is likely to do well through this site.

The site is hugely popular as it is one of the most effective book promotion sites. Many of the other sites has dubious results at best, but this one usually delivers. When you submit your book for a promotion, there is a chance that it won't be accepted initially. If it is rejected, then take on board any feedback they provide you and resubmit it at a later date. Some writers report getting a Bookbub deal on their first attempt whereas others report nothing but frustration as their book is constantly turned down.

In the more popular genres, they are swamped with writers wanting their book promoted, so often reject perfectly good books. Keep applying, keep gaining reviews and eventually you could be accepted. Don't take their rejection as a reflection on the quality of your book; it may be that they are overwhelmed with submissions in that category and so are rejected every submission.

This is something worth pursuing, particularly if you are a fiction author or you are writing in a more general nonfiction category. Be sitting down when you look at the price of the promotions as it isn't cheap, but it can be very effective. If you only have a single book published, then do not attempt to get a Bookbub deal. This works best if you have multiple books in the series and your readers can finish the promoted book and then buy more of your books. This is what fiction authors count on when promoting their books; the read through rate is where they make money.

Of course, from this promotion, you can also gain social media followers and newsletter subscribers, but typically the focus is purely on making sales and promoting your book. It is probably the best and most sought after book promotion service, and worth looking at when you have multiple books published.

Using Other Promotional Sites to Promote Your Books

As well as Bookbub, there are a whole host of other sites that you can use to promote your books. The majority of these sites are focused on fiction books and so will not be very effective for nonfiction writers. There are some that will promote nonfiction books, but they usually have very broad categories, if they have any category beyond nonfiction, which means there may not be much of a target audience for your books.

The cost of these promotional sites varies significantly and is not always related to performance. Unfortunately, with many of these sites, you have no way of tracking the results. You are unable to include tracking pixels or affiliate links so you can monitor how many clicks you get. The jury is definitely out on these promotional sites with some authors claiming they earned a fortune from them and other authors seeing no result whatsoever. For me, the lack of ability to track clicks makes most of these promotions dubious at best. You have no idea whether you are getting a return on your investment or whether the promotion has made you any money.

A Google search will reveal these sites as will asking a question on one of the many author related Facebook groups.

The best way to use these promotional sites is to run one promotion at a time, leaving several days between promotions. As you have a good idea of what your average daily sales are, you can spot any increases in sales or page reads of your books based on your Amazon reporting pages. This isn't ideal by any stretch of the imagination, but at least it gives you a good idea of whether or not the promotion has made its money back.

The cost of the site will vary and can be a hundred dollars or more. Typically, the cost is based on the number of people your book will be sent to and the response rate the site owner feels they will get.

These can be very effective, but can also produce poor results. I recommend looking at the experience of other authors on a site before you use it and see whether it has a specific category that your book falls into. If the categories are too broad and your book fits best into a narrow category, then you may struggle to make enough sales to cover your costs.

Some of these promotional sites can be very good, but their performance changes regularly, which is why I am not publishing a list of these sites. A quick search online will find plenty of these sites and then you need to research each one to determine how they are currently performing.

Book promotions are good to use around the launch of a new book. This drives people to the book, makes sales and helps boost it in the Amazon rankings. Don't book all your promotions on the same day, spread them out over a two to four week period. This means you get steady traffic to your book rather than a short burst of visitors. The sustained visits and purchases of your book will help your books more in the Amazon rankings than a quick burst of sales.

Bookbub is the holy grail of book promotion sites, but many other smaller sites are more affordable for the newer author. Remember to research the sites before you use them to ensure that they are going to be effective for your chosen niche. The performance of some of the smaller sites is very variable, so do your research before you spend your hard earned money.

Amazon Promotional Tools

Amazon provides two main tools to help you promote your book:

1. Free days
2. Countdown deals

These are both very good tools that you can use to help promote your books, particularly when used in conjunction with paid book promotions. Used wisely, these can be very good at getting your book noticed and helped your book climb up the Amazon rankings.

Free KDP Days and How to Use Them

In every 90 day period that your book is enrolled in the KDP Select program, you have five free promotion days that you can use. This allows you to give your book away for free.

What? Give your hard work away for free?

Calm down … Breathe … Let me explain.

These promotional days do not have to be used, but they can be used to give your book away to readers. If sales of a book are flagging, you want to try and get more reviews, or you have released another book in the series, then a free day can be very useful indeed.

When you launch a new book, then running a free day or two can be a very effective strategy to get your book 'out there' without having to spend a fortune on book promotions. I have run one or two days of free promotions when a book has been launched, which boosted the rankings of the book and then set it up for good sales after the free promotion ended. You can also tell how well a book will sell from how well it does on the free promotion days. If, when free, your book has a couple of dozen downloads then it isn't a particularly popular niche and is unlikely to sell a lot when people have to pay for it again. However, if you get several thousand downloads for your book when it is free, then your book is in a very popular niche and is likely to sell well when the promotion ends.

Typically, the majority of the free downloads will occur on the first day of the promotion. On the second day, you will see around half as many downloads and then from the third day onwards, free downloads grind to a halt. In my experience, running a free promotion works well, but should not be run for more than two days as the downloads on days three to five are minimal. You are better to run a second and even a third promotion in the ninety days if you are keen to use all of your promotional days, which you don't need to do.

You may think that free promotional days are doing to help you get reviews. Again, in my experience, books downloaded during a free promotion rarely get reviews. I am not sure why, but people who download books for free rarely leave reviews. It may be that people download the book simply because it is free.

One strategy that works well to boost your free downloads is to increase the price of your book just before the free day starts. Readers then see a more expensive book for free and are likely to think it is more of a deal to download. Think about it, if you see a $4.99 book for free you are more likely to download it, even out of curiosity, than a $0.99 book that is free. After the free days, you can price your book at the price point you had originally chosen.

Don't feel that you have to give your book away and use these days. Plenty of authors never touch them. However, when you are starting out and have a limited budget, the free promotion days can be a good way to get your book noticed and kick-start sales without having to spend a lot of money on promotions. As you build your social media following and newsletter, you will not need to use any free days as you can promote your new books to them instead.

Free days can be very useful when combined with book promotions, whether paid promotions as discussed in the previous chapter or promotions through your newsletter or social media. It depends upon your business strategy as to whether you use a free day or you use a countdown deal to discount your book. Some people prefer the former, so they maximize downloads, whereas other people prefer the latter so they recoup some or all of the costs of the promotion and get qualified buyers, i.e. People who are willing to spend money.

Create a new Free Book Deal

Choose when the promotion will start and end
Kindle Free Book Deal promotions can run for up to 5 days

Start Date   August 30, 2017   End Date   September 2, 2017

Free promotion days used: 4 / 5

Which you use is entirely up to you. Both approaches are perfectly valid and will work. Some people prefer the free book because then they can maximize their downloads with the aim of people then buying other books in the series. If you do not have a good read through rate or do not have multiple books, then the discounted approach can be better.

Permafree Books
Some authors will have books which are permafree. These are books which are permanently free to download. This is not done out of the kindness of their heart but is a sound business strategy when you have multiple books in the marketplace on the same or related subjects.

Readers download your book, enjoy the content and follow the links in it to your other books and then either buy it or read it on Kindle Unlimited.

This can be a very effective strategy when you have a series of books or some books on similar subjects. For example, if I was in the self-help niche, I may have books published on confidence, stress management, motivation, creativity, relaxation and goal setting. I would write a decent length book (10,000 to 20,000 words) on the general subject of self-help providing tips and strategies. Each of the subjects that I have a book on would be covered but in less detail and with one main strategy being covered. The book would contain references to the full-length books.

This can be used as a giveaway to your newsletter subscribers as an incentive to sign up for your list (but it could not be in KDP Select). As a permafree book on Amazon, readers would 'buy' it, enjoy the content and then they would check out your other books, either buying those or reading them on Kindle Unlimited.

Amazon does not like to list books for free, so the way to set up a permafree book is slightly complex. List your book on Amazon and give it a price of $2.99. You need to remove your free book from the KDP Select program. Once this is done, list the book on another site such as Nook or Kobo and set the price to $0.00. When the book is live, contact Amazon and tell them the book is available free elsewhere, giving them the link, and ask them to price match. They will do so, and your book is available for free!

When used properly, these free days can be a useful tool, but be careful about giving away a book that is selling well, unless it is part of a well thought out strategy. Think carefully about how you want to use these days and how they can benefit your business. They can help boost a flagging book and kick-start a new book, but be careful you do not de-value your book or upset buyers.

Countdown Deals and How to Use Them

Countdown deals are another very useful promotional tool that you can use. In a countdown deal, your original price is clearly displayed along with the discounted price and the amount of time left on the deal. The price will increase in increments, set by you until the deal has ended. You can just set a lower price and not let it increase incrementally.

The real benefit to you is that you retain your commission rate, even at lower prices. This means that your $4.99 book will pay 70% commission when sold at $0.99 rather than the 35% commission you should receive. Obviously, this means you get twice the commission, so you don't mind running a deal together with a big promotion.

When using a countdown deal with a promotion, you need to ensure you give Amazon plenty of notice to set up the deal. It can take up to 72 hours for a countdown deal to go live, and many an author has been caught out by changing the price at the last minute. Often changes are approved much faster, but be aware of the potential time scale.

Another benefit of a countdown deal is that Amazon has set up a website specifically for countdown deals, www.amazon.com/kindlecountdowndeals. Here they list all of the books on countdown so readers can find good deals. This alone will help you get a bit of a boost in your sales as new buyers find your books and give them a try because they are on offer.

A countdown deal can run for a maximum of 7 days and can be run on either Amazon.com or Amazon.co.uk.

1. Select marketplace.

Kindle Countdown Deals are configured by marketplace. You can schedule one Kindle Countdown Deal in each available KDP Select term.

Marketplace   Amazon.com ÷

2. Choose when the promotion will start and end.

Kindle Countdown Deal promotions can run for up to 7 days

Must be after August 31, 2017 (Why?)

Start   August 31, 2017

8:00 AM ÷   PST

Must be before November 18, 2017 (Why?)

End   September 6, 2017

12:00 AM ÷   PST

Let's say your book normally sells for $4.99 and you want to run a countdown deal over four days with the price increasing every 24 hours. You start the deal at 8 am on Monday morning. The deal would look something like this:

- Monday at 8 am – The book is on sale at $0.99
- Tuesday at 8 am – The book price increases to $1.99
- Wednesday at 8 am – The book price increases to $2.99
- Thursday at 8 am – The book returns to its original price of $4.99

Here's an illustration from Amazon of a countdown deal on a $2.99 book running over a week.

Increment		Duration	Price	% Discount
1	August 31, 2017 at 8:00 AM (PST)	68h	$0.99	67%
2	September 3, 2017 at 4:00 AM (PST)	68h	$1.99	34%
End	September 6, 2017 at 12:00 AM (PST)		Original list price $2.99	

When you are running a promotion, whether on social media, to a newsletter or a paid promotion, you can see how this can encourage people to make the purchase. People who have never heard of you are far more likely to give your book a go at $0.99, and then you hope they will buy further books you have published and follow you on social media.

Countdown deals are a very good way of promoting your book without giving it away for free. Once you are established in the market and have a good following, using countdown deals with new books is an excellent way for you to gain traction and make sales when the book is launched. It represents a good deal for your current readers, helps encourage new readers to try your book and boosts your ranking within Amazon.

AMAZON MARKETING SERVICES (AMS) ADVERTISING

Amazon provides a method for you to advertise your books on their site. At present, this is only available for Amazon.com, but it will be introduced to the United Kingdom soon and, hopefully, rolled out to the rest of the Amazon sites not long after.

You can only use AMS advertising if you have published your book as a Kindle book, through the KDP platform. If you have used a third party publisher such as Pronoun or Draft2Digital, then you will not be able to use AMS advertising for your books.

This advertising platform can be found by either going to http://ams.amazon.com or by clicking the Promote and Advertise option next to any book in your KDP control panel and choosing Create an Ad Campaign.

There are two types of advert you can use on Amazon:

1. Sponsored Products
2. Product Display Ad

Although the principles are the same for both types of advert, there is a slight difference between them. A Sponsored Product ad is displayed in a box with other products whereas a Product Display Ad only shows your product and no others.

The response rate between the two varies according to a wide number of factors, though the latter typically requires a higher budget, but gets a good response rate because your product is not lost within a host of other products.

Bids & Budgets

Both types of adverts require you to set a bid for each click and an overall budget, usually a daily budget. This is how much money you are willing to spend each day on your advertising. Remember this is per day and it will be multiplied by the number of days in the month for your total bill. However, in all but the most competitive niches, you are not going to hit this daily budget. This amount influences how many clicks per day you will get. You may not spend your entire daily budget; it depends on your bid per click and how many times your ad is displayed.

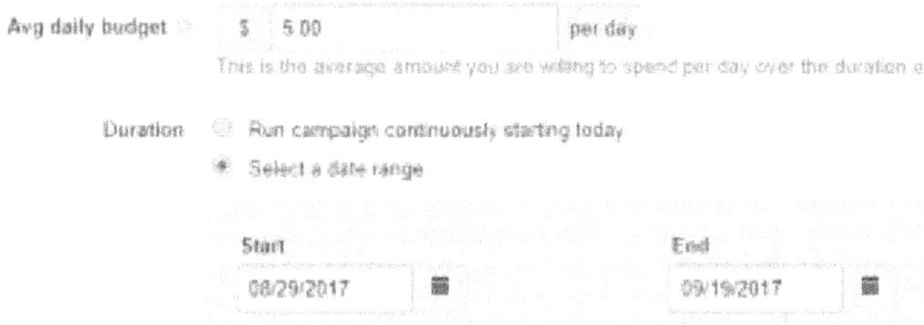

The maximum bid per click is how much you will pay for each click on your advert and can be set to anything from $0.01 upwards. Divide your daily budget by your bid per click to work out the maximum number of clicks you will get per day. How much you pay for each click will vary depending on the other advertisers you are bidding against. You may end up paying less than your maximum bid per click.

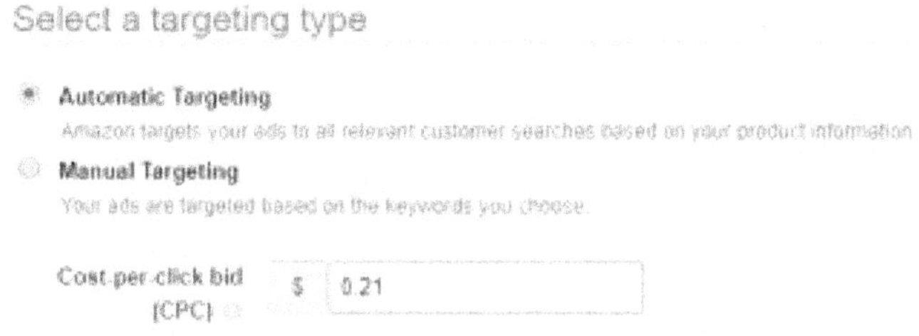

How much your maximum bid per click will be depends on a wide variety of factors, though mainly it is based on how competitive your niche is. The more people that are trying to advertise products in your niche, the higher the cost per click will be.

The best approach is to start with a low bid and work your way up until you get an acceptable number of click throughs per day. Be prepared in the more competitive niches to pay a lot more than $0.25 per click.

If you have written a series of books, then you are best running AMS ads for the first book so that readers will buy that, enjoy it and then read your other books. If you are releasing a new book in a series, then you can advertise that and people will want to find out more about your other books.

Reporting

AMS offers some reporting functionality but, and I'll be honest here, it will drive you mad. At the time of writing, figures are delayed by as much as three days. This means that you can see your costs rising and not see any sales and all of a sudden some sales will appear. It makes it very hard to determine whether or not adverts are working. My advice is to run adverts for a couple of weeks without touching them to see how they are performing.

You can set your adverts to run for a pre-determined period or continually. I recommend starting by running your adverts for two weeks at a time until you have got your cost per click optimized, then you can run them for longer. AMS ads tend to trail off and perform worse over time, so I run my adverts for a month at a time, monitor them and tweak them as necessary. Amazon provides a very handy copy facility that allows you to copy an ad in its entirety. You can also change the end date of your adverts, allowing you to extend ads that are performing well without having to copy them and go through the review process again.

The AMS reports will show you how many impressions your advert has got. You are not paying per impression but per click, so don't be alarmed if this number runs into the tens of thousands. You can also see the number of clicks you get, which will be very low when compared to the number of impressions. Working on targeting better keywords and improving your ad copy can increase the number of clicks you get.

You can also see your aCPC or average cost per click. This tells you how much, on average, you are paying per click, which helps you manage your bid per click.

Impressions	Clicks	aCPC	Spend	Est. Total Sales	ACoS
16,081	22	$0.11	$2.37	$0.00	0
13,574	23	$0.14	$3.20	$2.99	107.02%
–	–	–	$0.00	–	0
70,533	106	$0.09	$9.93	$26.95	36.85%
50,967	133	$0.12	$16.27	$55.09	29.53%

As well as this, AMS show you your spend on that advert plus your estimated total sales, which is often very slow to update. These figures are useful as they are used to help determine the profitability of the advert. You need to be aware that you cannot determine the read through rate for people buying other books in your series too.

The interesting figure is the ACoS or average cost of sale. This is expressed as a percentage and gives you an idea of whether or not an advert is profitable just based on Kindle book sales. When the figure is 100%, it means that you are spending as much on the advert as you are making. The lower the figure, the better, but remember it does not take into account page reads, physical book sales or read through, so you need to monitor all of your figures to determine if an ad is profitable.

It is not unheard of for an advert to be showing an ACOS in excess of 100%, but is making a huge profit from physical book sales and read through to other books in a series.

The one downside of this reporting is that it does not take into account physical book sales or page reads on KDP Select. The former may well be introduced when Amazon has fully integrated CreateSpace into KDP, though when the latter will be introduced is anyone's guess.

This poor reporting makes it extremely difficult to determine if an advert is performing well. You may see that your advert is performing dreadfully according to the AMS reporting, but your page reads or physical book sales could be increased significantly because of the ads. However, there is no way of knowing for sure apart from stopping the ads and seeing if these sales or page reads decrease.

Creating Ad Text

The ad text itself can be anything up to 150 characters in length. Be aware that Amazon police this text militantly, so don't include claims such as best-selling or anything similar without providing solid proof to Amazon. Also, they do not like initial capitals on all of the words. Their requirements change and can even vary from reviewer to reviewer. Write the best advert you can, submit it for review and you'll soon get feedback on whether or not it is suitable.

Your ad text needs to grab your readers attention and get them to click on the ad. It will be displayed next to your book cover and below the title and author. I would recommend looking at other adverts in your niche to see what they are using to inspire you and give you ideas on what is working. This will vary a lot depending on whether you are writing young adult books, nonfiction or any other type of book. The basics of advertising apply in that your ad copy needs to get attention and make the reader want to find out more. I recommend a one sentence description that makes excites your reader about your book and feel like they are missing out if they don't read it.

Sponsored Product Ads

These are the most commonly used adverts and are very easy to set up. You set your average daily budget, a duration for your advert and then how you are going to target your advert.

It is targeted either automatically or manually. Once you have chosen this, you set your cost per click bid, enter your ad copy and then submit your ad for approval, which can take anything up to 72 hours.

Automatic targeting of your ad means that Amazon decides on where to advertise your book rather than you telling it. This works very well for nonfiction and less well for fiction books. Amazon looks at your book description and determines from this what products to advertise your book on.

Manual targeting is best for fiction books as you enter a list of keywords that you want to target. These are keywords relating to your niche and, in the case of fiction, the names of popular authors in your genre and their books, particularly popular, new releases. You can set an individual cost per click bid for each keyword so that you can pay more for the best performing keywords and less for the less competitive keywords.

This type of targeting is best if you want to specifically target keywords and display your ads to a target audience. This can be very effective, but on some nonfiction books, it can be hard gathering a sufficient list of keywords, in which case automatic targeting is better to use. I have found automatic targeting to work extremely well with nonfiction books and gets an excellent response rate. I suppose it is easy for Amazon to determine what a nonfiction book is about and so display the adverts on pages of related products.

Product Display Ads

Product Display Ads are set up in a similar way to Sponsored Product Ads in relation to the cost per click and budget.

The key difference between the two types of advert is how they are targeted. The Product Display Ads are targeted either by product or interest.

Product targeting allows you to either target specific products or target related categories. Targeting by interest allows you to choose different interests, based on Amazon categories.

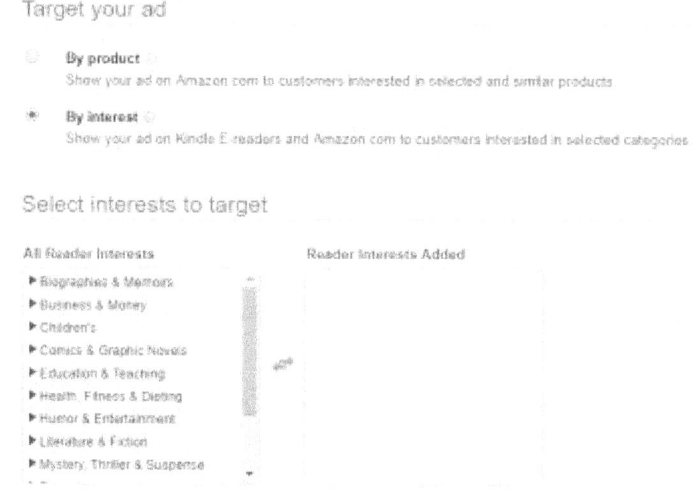

You can only select product or interest targeted, not both for an advert. If you want to use both, then you will need to set up two adverts one using product targeting and one using interest targeting.

This type of advert is very good and can be used in conjunction with a Sponsored Product Ad. Many authors will use both types of advert to advertise their books.

Making Your Adverts Profitable

This is the holy grail for an author and the part that makes many pull their hair out in frustration. The advertising isn't perfect, and the delay in reporting is incredibly annoying.

Making your advert profitable means that you need to get the balance right on your cost per click bid and your book pricing. Books priced below $2.99 are extremely difficult to advertise and make a profit from the initial sales. However, some people will advertise a 99c book, making a loss on the initial sale because they know they will profit from the read through.

You need to adjust your cost per click bid until you have a sufficient number of clicks every day without blowing your budget. Ideally, your adverts should at least pay for themselves, if not make a profit.

Run two or three adverts with different ad copy to see how the ad copy affects performance. Simply create a single advert and then copy it and change the ad copy. You may find that different ad copy increases the click through rate significantly.

AMS adverts are a definite must for any author. You don't have to spend thousands of dollars every month on advertising. Initially you can spend under a hundred to test your adverts, make them profitable and then scale up the advertising.

These are great to run when you are launching a new book as it can get eyeballs on your book much faster than if you just launch it and hope for the best.

I put off using AMS for a long time because I was unsure about it and didn't want to risk the money. Eventually, some author buddies bullied me into trying it, and I was utterly amazed by the results. Just using automatic targeting, I was making six times the amount I was spending on advertising, just from the initial sale, not including read throughs, physical books or page reads. I now use AMS whenever I launch a book as it helps it make sales from day one without spending a fortune on advertising. AMS ads turned my least profitable book sale months into the most profitable months I ever had, and I will continue to use them because they help make sales.

WHEN & HOW TO HIRE A VA

At some point in your writing career, you may get to a stage where you want or need to hire a virtual assistant to take on some of the day to day tasks of your business, leaving you to concentrate on the actual writing part.

This can be a very liberating experience for you, but you need to understand exactly what the VA will do for you and manage their time. Of course, the cost of your virtual assistant is a tax deductible expense.

A VA can help you with a wide variety of tasks including:

- Managing social media
- Writing web content
- Managing web sites
- Customer service duties
- Research

And anything else you need help with. Some will be able to design book covers, write blurb, publish your books for you and even write your books too!

Hiring a VA can be a difficult process because you need to understand what you want a VA to do before you can hire one. Typically, your VA will be in the Far East and, depending on what you are paying, can do anything from basic research to running a big part of your business for you. The more expensive VA's tend to be the ones with the greater experience and abilities.

As your VA will probably have English as a second language, you need to ensure that their language skills are of a level which you find suitable. From experience, most of them have a good command of English, but you need to give precise instructions. If your instructions do not make sense or miss out vital steps, then you can expect problems. Clearly communicate what you expect regarding activity, working hours, communication, and so on, and confirm that they understand what you want.

Virtual assistants can be found on some of the freelancing sites such as www.upwork.com, www.freelancer.com and many more. The advantage of hiring someone through a freelancing site is you can often see feedback from other people they have worked for which gives you an idea of the quality of their work. Often as this is the main source of their income, you know they are going to genuinely do the best they can for you because they need positive feedback on the site to continue to get work.

A freelancer can be hired for one day a week, a couple of days a week or full time, depending on your needs. You can start a freelancer off for a day a week to help out with some jobs and then as your need grows and their skills improve, you can increase the amount of time you have them working for you.

Depending on the skill level of the VA, they can cost anything from a couple of dollars upwards an hour. You get what you pay for with a VA, and the more expensive ones are well worth the money for the skills, English ability, and helpfulness.

You can hire a VA from a Western European country or the USA, but you need to be aware that these are going to be significantly more expensive because of the cost of living. Two bucks an hour is a pittance in the USA that no-one can live on, but in Bangladesh, it is an extremely good wage. I know of authors who have university graduates with a degree in English working for them for $10 an hour writing books and researching content.

When you find yourself spending more time on mundane tasks that anyone could do, then you need to look at hiring a VA. Look at the jobs you are doing within your business and determine which of these can be done by someone else compared to which can only be done by you.

Researching recipe ideas for a book can be done by anyone, but re-writing the content may be something that you feel only you can do. Posting to social media and managing your website may be consuming more and more time that could be better be spent writing instead. Often, as your business grows, you get caught up in doing mundane, day-to-day tasks and less time writing the books that make you the money.

Start by hiring a VA for a day or two a week and then gradually increase it as your income increases and your need increases. The great thing about hiring a VA from Asia is that they are starting work as you are going to bed and finishing when you get up. They are perfect for research because they effectively work when you sleep, and you wake up the next morning to have the information you need to work on during the day.

Not everyone will need to hire a VA, but if you find you are struggling to find enough time to write because you are doing other things instead, then it is time to hire help. Of course, you don't need to hire a virtual assistant; you may find someone locally who you can employ or even a family member. Be aware that hiring locally is different to hiring virtually and you may be responsible for providing employee benefits, paying taxes, sick pay, holiday pay, maternity leave and more. The simplicity of hiring a virtual assistant attracts many writers who do not need a local personal assistant.

HOW TO OVERCOME WRITER'S BLOCK

Writer's block is something that will strike many authors at some point in their career. Overcoming it can be difficult as it can literally cripple a writer, preventing them from finishing a book. Over time you will learn when writer's block is approaching and tactics that work for you to get rid of it.

This can be caused by many different factors including:

- Boredom – when you have been working on a book for months or even years, you can get fed up with it on a conscious or sub-conscious level and block yourself from continuing to write

- Timing – perhaps it isn't quite the right time in your life to write, or other things demand your attention. Sometimes, ideas need time to stew before they are ready to be committed to paper

- Fear – this is very common with a lot of new authors and can be a fear of failure or, more insidiously, a fear of success. You will be surprised how many authors block their writing because they are frightened it won't be enjoyed by readers, or they are scared of actually succeeding and being a successful author. The latter usually results in self-sabotage of some sort and a great deal of procrastination

- Perfectionism – also very common, more so with new authors. It's the need to get your book perfect which results in a struggle to write because you cannot make the words as perfect as the image in your head

There is no defined way to cure writer's block; it is a very individual process. Some of the methods that I've found work for my fellow authors and for me include:

- Going for a walk or doing something in nature such as gardening – this helps to relax your mind and get it in focus again
- Take some exercise – again; this gets your blood flowing and focuses your mind
- Eliminate distractions – if you are finding yourself wasting time on Facebook or pointless websites, switch the Internet off. Get rid of whatever is distracting you so you can focus on writing
- Change your environment – pick your laptop up and go and write somewhere else. A change of scenery can often help overcome writer's block. I find sitting outside or going to a café helps me get focused again. The act of being in new surroundings seems to help clear writer's block
- Write something else – sometimes it isn't time to write your book. I tend to have two or three books on the go at any one time, which isn't for everyone I hasten to add. I will work on one and then, when I find myself struggling, I move to another and then return to the first when the block has gone. This works for me writing nonfiction, but fiction authors can find this difficult. If you are a fiction author, then you can write a short story set in your universe, write back stories for some characters or something similar if you don't want to distract yourself with a new story
- Put on some music – this can help you gain some clarity and focus
- Get into a writing routine – conditioning your body to write at certain times can help eliminate writer's block. If you condition yourself by starting to write at 9 am, stopping at 12 pm, starting again at 1 pm and then finishing at 4 pm your brain will get used to this routine and perform during those hours. Just knowing that you have time off from writing can help prevent writer's block. Writing at random times often prevents you from focusing because your brain is worrying that it will have to stop shortly to do something else

These are just a few ideas that work for most people. I've heard many other stories from authors on how they overcome the dreaded writer's block including one author who has a box of Lego in his office. When writer's block hits, he gets the Lego out and builds things which gets rid of the block.

The 'cure' varies from person to person and as you get into the habit of writing more, so you will find what works for you and what doesn't. You may find you struggle to write when you are worrying about things such as work, jobs around the house and so on. Often taking care of the things that are causing the block will get you writing again.

There are some activities though that authors have found do not help cure writer's block, even though many people use them! Watching TV typically does nothing to get you writing again as it is a form of excuse and procrastination to avoid putting pen to paper. Deciding you are not going to write until you are 'inspired' is another big, fat excuse; it may be months or years before that inspiration hits by which time you've missed the boat! This is yet another excuse you make to yourself to procrastinate about writing your book, usually down to fear of success or failure.

Absolutely the best way to overcome writer's block is actually to write. Just write something, maybe rewrite part of your book, write a few lines, proof read some of your book, anything. Sometimes you literally have to force your way through the block, break down the wall and keep on going. Over time you will get to know yourself and know when to push through it and when to take a break, though make sure that break doesn't become an extended vacation! I know of authors who have 'taken a break' because of writer's block and come back to their book years later or scrapped it completely!

If you want to make a business out of this, then you are going to have to learn to deal with writer's block and push through it. Yes, writing is an art, but it also puts food on your table. If you are not writing, then you are not earning. You can keep making excuses and procrastinate, or you can knuckle down, get writing and push through. I know there are times when writing even a sentence is like squeezing blood from a stone, but I find if I keep pushing, write a couple of sentences or paragraphs then suddenly I'm back in the flow and able to write again.

This can be a real struggle for many people, and sometimes you need to force yourself through it if nothing else works. I was writing a book on a subject which required some specialist knowledge and some mathematics in it. It took me over a year to finish that book because I balked at learning enough about the subject to write about it properly. When I eliminated distractions and forced myself to learn the subject, it took about three hours to get my head around the topic. Then I easily finished the rest of it, which went on to become one of my bestselling books.

This is a very real problem which you need to work out a solution for that works for you. It is likely to strike you some time in your writing career. You will notice it when you find yourself procrastinating about writing, making excuses as to why you cannot write, finding reasons to do other things or even wasting your writing time surfing the Internet or playing games. Take action to get through it and don't use it as an excuse to quit!

AVOIDING THE COMMON MISTAKES WRITERS MAKE

There are some common mistakes people make when they start to write a book. These can affect any author, and they could end up making one, two or more of these mistakes, or even making none of them.

I'd like to take a few minutes and share with you the common issues authors face and give you some tips and advice to overcome these problems Writing isn't always plain sailing, and this section will help you get past some of the most frequently found problems.

Too Many Projects
You've started a book, now you've decided you are going to be an author. The problem is, you are full of ideas and excited about them all, so you start working on each idea as soon as it hits.

The result? A hard drive full of part written books!

The best way to get around this problem is to take the new ideas, outline them briefly in a paragraph or two and keep them in a file on your computer or in a notebook. Focus on a single idea at a time, or have a couple of books on the go so you can overcome writer's block.

When I first started writing, I suffered from this problem. I ended up with close to twenty part written books on my computer where I had had a good idea, started writing and then got distracted by a new idea. I realized I was making no money because I wasn't publishing anything!

My solution was easy; I created a document in which I kept my ideas for new books. I would focus on finishing a single book and then move on to the next one that excited me. It took a few months, but I eventually finished most of those twenty books; a couple were discarded as they were not viable subjects.

The same applies to taking part in writing competitions, boxed sets and so on. Be careful about taking on too much and becoming overwhelmed, so you don't complete anything.

Lack of Organization in a Book

Readers like a well-organized book, particularly in nonfiction. Your book has to flow and follow a logical structure. If it jumps all over the place and you have advanced information before presenting basic information, then it is going to annoy the reader.

Before you start writing, outline the chapters of your book and how the information is going to flow. Even nonfiction is telling a story; the story of solving the problem that made the reader pick up the book in the first place.

A book that flows logically will get much better reviews and be well received by your readers. Think carefully about how you are going to organize your book, and don't be afraid to change it if you feel it can be done better.

Poor Working Environment

This is a problem that affects most Indie authors, particularly when they start out. If your working environment is not conducive to writing, then you are going to struggle to produce good quality books.

Perhaps you write on a laptop on your knee in the evening, while you watch television. This is not ideal, and it will reflect in your writing as you make mistakes and even (yes, I've done this) include dialog from the TV show in your book without realizing it.

It won't always be possible to have a perfect working environment. You may not have room in your home for a desk, or have to work while other people are around who may disturb you. Try to set up the best possible working environment you can, eliminating as many distractions as possible.

You will find you are far more productive from an hour in a good working environment compared to three hours in a poor working environment.

Scheduling Writing Time

A lot of Indie authors will write as and when they can when they first start out. While this may be necessary, you can find it difficult to get in the mood to write.

Schedule regular writing time and stick to it, avoiding excuses to put it off. The reason behind this is that you condition yourself to be in the mood for writing at that time and are more productive.

The time you schedule will depend on your lifestyle. I used to get up at 5:30 am and spend an hour writing before I had to get ready for work. I found that hour to be more productive than any other time I spent writing because I was used to writing then. Yes, it was a struggle initially, but I soon started to look forward to this time.

Think about how you can schedule time for writing, even if it is just an hour a day. One hour every day is better than trying to find several hours all together once or twice a week. An hour is easy for anyone to find and you will make huge strides towards becoming an author if you spend this time regularly writing.

Lack of Writing Tools
This can be a huge problem for many Indie authors. I know people who write books on their cell phone because they don't have anything else to write on. Having the right tools means that writing is much easier. This doesn't mean you need to go out and spend a fortune on equipment. It means you need to determine what you need to write and get your hands on that equipment.

Most of us will use a Windows PC, though Apple Mac computers are much sought after by writers even though they are hideously expensive. If you can afford it, then you can use Microsoft Office to write, but that requires a one off payment or a monthly subscription. Alternatively, you can use Google Docs, which is free. On an Apple, people use software such as Scrivener, but that isn't cheap either.

As all you are doing is writing, you don't need a super computer to be productive. Yes, it is nice having the latest, fastest laptop, but anything that can run a word processor will do to start with. Buy the expensive computer when you have the money coming in from your books.

Second-hand computers that are capable of running an older version of Microsoft Word or Google Docs can be bought very cheaply or even gained for free. Perhaps a friend or family member is upgrading their computer and will give you their old one for free.

Look at buying a Google Chromebook as they are very cheap and will run

Google Docs. They aren't good for much other than using the Internet, but you can write a book on them.

Think carefully about what tools you need to make your writing life easier. Initially, you may have to make do with less than ideal tools, but identify what you need and put your publishing profits towards them.

Failing to Backup Work

Your business and your income comes from your books. Where are you storing them?

On your laptop? What happens if you drop your laptop tomorrow and it stops working?

What do you do? Make a panic post to an author group on Facebook? Cry? Both of these and more?

Backing up your work is absolutely vital. I cannot stress to you enough how important this is. Do not think that by keeping your work on a USB stick or an external hard drive means it is backed up. Only yesterday I saw someone post on a Facebook group in despair because their USB stick was mysteriously blank and several years of work had vanished. No, the author in question didn't have any other backups, having felt that keeping their entire business on a single USB stick was a great idea!

My recommendation is to have a main location where you work from. This is where you keep your work in progress and open files you are working on, otherwise you may get confused and edit the wrong version. Keeping track of which file you are working on is essential otherwise you end up with bits of the book in different files, and it is hard to pull it all together.

Then back this up to a cloud service such as Google Drive, Apple iCloud or Microsoft OneDrive. Which one you use does not matter as they all do pretty much the same thing. I would not use any service offered by a third party as you never know how long they will be in business.

Once a week, on the same day, so it becomes a habit, back all of your files up to a USB stick and put that away somewhere safe. You never touch this stick, it is purely used for backups. Ideally, create three folders on it and keep three different versions of your data, overwriting the oldest one each time you backup.

My personal solution is to use Microsoft OneDrive. This is where I keep all of my work in progress, and I can access it from any device I choose to use to write on. This is automatically replicated to my desktop and my laptop by OneDrive itself; I don't need to do anything to ensure my files are safe. Every week I copy these files on to my USB stick which is hidden away in the back of my desk drawer for safety, and so no one else accidentally uses it. That USB stick is never used for anything else. This solution works and keeps my files safe. Unfortunately, I have lost my files not once, but twice when laptops and external hard drives have died, so I am now extremely cautious about protecting my business.

A pricey alternative is to buy a RAID 5 Network Attached Storage (NAS) device. This has redundant hard drives so that if one fails you do not lose your data and attaches to your network at home. They are very good and worth it if you are serious about keeping your data safe.

Not Researching Title and Keywords

These are important for your book to stand out from the crowd and be found by Amazon's search algorithms. Unfortunately, many new authors will ignore the technical aspect of these and choose titles and, worse, keywords, out of thin air without actually knowing if they are going to help their books get listed.

With fiction books, the title is not as important, but for a nonfiction book, the title is extremely important in helping you get eyeballs on your book. The title of a nonfiction book influences how your book is found in the search results and whether a reader knows the book is relevant to them.

Do not pluck keywords out of the air, research them and choose the keywords that not only best fit your book, but are ones that people are searching for on Amazon. It will help you get your books found. You will only have to re-do this step later on if you skip it at the start and it can be too late to change the title then.

Poor Quality Book Cover

A book is judged by its cover, no matter what the proverb says. If your cover is not up to scratch, then your book sales are going to struggle. Many new authors will try to save money on the cover either by hiring a cheap, poor quality designer or doing the cover themselves. This is going to impact your ability to earn money from your books seriously!

You don't have to spend a fortune on your book covers, but you do need to get good quality covers. If you cannot afford an original, hand drawn cover for your fiction book then get one that uses blended stock photos, it will be much cheaper. Nonfiction book covers are very affordable and can be bought for between five and ten bucks on Fiverr.

Badly Written Blurb

Your blurb sells your books, and you will be surprised how many people have poorly written blurb or blurb full of spelling mistakes and grammatical errors.

This book description not only tells people about your book, but it also informs them of the quality of your book. If the description is bad, what does that say about the book? Would you buy a book where there are spelling mistakes in the description?

Make sure your blurb is well written, describes your book and entices your reader to buy your book or at least use the Look Inside facility. Spell and grammar check it. If you find you are struggling with it, then get a professional to proof read and edit it.

If You Write It, They Will Buy It

Wrong! No, people will not just buy your book if you write and publish it. You need to actively promote your book whether on social media, advertising or through book promotions.

If you do not actively promote your book, then you will struggle to make sales. Remember there are hundreds of thousands, if not millions, of books on Amazon vying for the attention of readers. Your book can very easily get lost in the crowd unless you promote it.

Many authors consider writing the book the easiest part of being a writer. The hard work starts once you hit the publish button and have to promote your book, so it earns its keep.

Lack of Understand of Target Market

You need to understand who you are writing your book for. Different markets have different requirements, and if you do not understand what your target market wants, then you are going to struggle to make sales. The book will not go down well and may struggle to get decent reviews.

Understand the needs of your target market, particularly with nonfiction. What problems do they need solving? What are the common problems encountered in the niche? What clever ways are there for solving these problems?

Give your market what they are looking for, and they will be happy.

Failure to Stick to Genre Tropes

As we just mentioned, nonfiction readers expect to be understood by an author, but so do fiction readers. The difference is that in fiction, understanding your target market means understanding the tropes that are expected in your genre.

Different genres have different expectations. Think about any genre of writing, and there will be common points between them. Young adult, dystopian books tend to have a young, female character as the main character. Often they will be the 'chosen one' and be living in a broken future, usually caused by war. There is likely to be a love triangle, with the main character being interested in one potential suitor and the other seeming much nicer and better for her, but she can't see that.

The list goes on, and every genre has these tropes. Readers expect these tropes, and if books do not conform enough, they get very upset and will leave negative reviews! You can often ignore one or maybe two of the tropes, so long as you stick firmly to the rest, but be careful, you do not upset your readers too much.

A lot of new writers are not aware of tropes, but they are required for all genres. Research the tropes for your chosen genre and make sure that you write in those required to keep your readers happy.

Poor Proof Reading and Editing

This is probably the biggest let down in Indie books. Many new authors do not have the funds to pay for proof reading and editing. This cost will run into the hundreds of dollars and can be a stretch too much for an author on a budget.

However, if your book is poorly edited and full of spelling mistakes, then you are going to get negative reviews. If you read negative reviews on a lot of Indie books, you will see that the quality of editing is the number one criticism.

If you cannot afford to hire a professional, then get some friends to read it over in exchange for a few beers and a barbeque. Spend $29.95 for a one-month subscription to Grammarly and run your book through that. There are ways to get your book proof read without spending a fortune. Once you are making the big bucks, then every book must be professionally edited, and proof read. It will make a huge difference in quality and how your readers receive your book.

Turning Writing into a Full-Time Income

Some authors are lucky, and they hit a home run with their first book. These authors, though, are the exception, rather than the rule. Many authors release their first book with a sense of elation only to be deflated when it doesn't fly off the virtual shelves.

Making a full-time income from writing consists of two key components:

1. Consistent promotion
2. Writing lots of books

At the end of the day, writing is a numbers game. It is quite easy to write a book that will make you $1 a day. Sure, that's not going to make you rich, but what if you have ten books doing that? Ten bucks a day, which pays for your coffee and daily newspaper.

What if you managed to make $5 a day from a book through advertising and CreateSpace sales, which is very easy to do. Ten books now make you $50 a day which is nice, but not a full-time income, it's only $18,250 a year, but how much of a difference would that extra money make to your life?

Five dollars a day is surprisingly easy to make with a nonfiction book that is well researched and well written without a huge amount of promotion.

Imagine if you had fifty books on the market, each one is making you $5 a day. This will bring you in $91,250 per year. Can you imagine how different your life would be if you had this income every year on auto-pilot?

Sounding good now?

What if your books made, on average, $10 a day? What if you had a hundred books? What if your books averaged $20 a day?

You can see that this is a numbers game. It is about identifying markets, writing a book for that market and then promoting the hell out of it. Once your book gets traction it can often retain it and make sales on its own.

When you properly research your niche, identify the content your readers want to see and then write a high-quality book, you will start to make money. The first couple of books may not make a lot of money for you. Over time, as you improve your writing and marketing skills, you will find that you are better able to identify profitable markets and produce high-quality books.

Producing books comes down to time to write at the end of the day. If you have a couple of hours a week, then it will take you longer to produce books than if you can write a couple of hours a day. Look at how you can increase your writing time so that you can produce more books.

The beauty of nonfiction writing is that you can outsource the writing very easily. You can either hire someone to write the entire book, or you can hire people to write articles which will become chapters. You then pull the chapters together to turn them into a coherent book.

Depending on the quality of writing, you can expect to pay as little as $200 for ten thousand words as a book. A thousand word article could cost you anything from $10 to $15, or more for a higher quality writer. Realistically, you can get a twenty thousand word book written as articles for about $200.

Some nonfiction authors will concentrate their time on researching niches and producing tables of content. These are then sent to writers who will produce the books for them, which are then published on Amazon. This is a very quick way to get a lot of books written, but you need to be able to identify profitable niches and manage your writers.

Whether or not you write books yourself or outsource them is up to you. If you are writing the books yourself, then look at how you can increase the time you spend writing so you can produce more books.

Realistically, writing full time, you can produce a 20,000 to 40,000 high quality, well research book in two weeks working eight hours a day, five days a week. It requires discipline as not everyone can work at home without being distracted. Working like this you can produce 26 books every year.

Remember that October to December will usually see a big increase in sales, often seeing increases as high as five to eight times normal sales.

You can make this a full-time income, but you need to have a plan and decide how you are going to scale it up. A single book may make some money, it may make no money, or you may hit it out of the park and make a lot of money from it. It comes down to how you research your niches and the quality of your books.

ENDNOTE

More and more people are unhappy with their jobs or seek extra income, usually through side jobs to help them make ends meet in an increasingly expensive and uncertain world. Perhaps they take a second job or start a home business, or maybe they start to write books.

The beauty of writing books is that once they are written, you make money on that book regardless of whether you work or not. I wrote a book two years ago; it makes about $400 a month whether or not I do anything. If I run adverts then the sales increase, but it ticks over at more or less that figure every month, and setting up ads doesn't take very long. This book has been earning for two years and will likely continue to earn for years to come.

Can you get that from a home business or a job? No, you trade time for money, and you are limited in how much you can earn by how much time you have. You cannot work more than 24 hours in a day and so cannot be paid for more than 24 hours. Try working 24 hours a day for a few days, and you'll soon fall to pieces. As a writer, you are no longer trading your time for money and so are gaining a freedom few employees have.

Writing is a long term game, where you are slowly building a portfolio of books until you have enough to make a full-time income.

With everything you have learned in this book, you know how to research niches, what readers are looking for and how to produce a high-quality book. Put into practice everything you have learned and you will be able to create a book that makes money, not just once, but day, after day, after day; year after year. The great thing about nonfiction books is that a lot of them are evergreen, meaning they will continue to sell for years. Fiction, although you can hit the big time from a single series or film deal, is more fickle as the popularity of genres wax and wane. Your bestselling fiction series could be dead in the water in six months.

Writing a book is about just that, writing. Many people want to be authors, and many people will tell you they'd love to write a book. It isn't difficult to do; you just have to sit in front of a computer and write. It is much easier now than in the past where you had to hand write it or use a typewriter. However, it comes down to putting word after word and creating your book.

Following through the process outlined in this book will allow you to create a nonfiction book that is going to sell. I've told you everything you need to know, but you are the one that has to write the book.

Identify a good niche, research the niche thoroughly and then produce the best quality book in that niche. After this, market it like crazy.

Studies have identified a strong online presence is vital to the success of an Indie author. I cannot stress how important this is to you in your marketing efforts. Start building a social media presence in your niche as soon as you decide what niche you are writing about. Then, when your book is launched, you will have an audience to market it to, which should kick start the sales from day one.

Becoming a full-time author is a very liberating experience as you realize the freedom it can give you. How many jobs will allow you to work the hours that suit you from the location that suits you? When my son was in the hospital I used to work evenings and on the train to the hospital, spending the day at his bedside. Now, I write every day, but if I want to take a day trip out with the family, I down tools and off I go, no asking anyone if it is convenient and whether I can take time off. I often take my iPad to my allotment and sit out in the sun working, which I find inspiring.

You can become a full-time author and make an awesome income from it. There are Indie authors who are making hundreds of thousands and even millions of dollars every year. I personally know authors who are making high five figure sums every month from their book sales! These authors regularly get ten million page reads a month! This adds up to a lot of money just from page reads.

It comes down to following the process that you have learned in this book and applying it. This last point is where most people fall down. Time and time again I see people saying it has taken them three years to finish a book.

That is fine if you are doing it for love, but if you want to make money, you must write faster than that.

Research your niches, identify a subject to write about, research and start writing. Get your book written and published. You will be surprised how enjoyable it is when you get started and how much you can write when you put your mind to it.

When you see your first sale and get the first payment into your bank account, you will be hooked. I check my book sales every day and love seeing the figure increasing. It gives me a real thrill and motivates me to keep writing. I often compare last month to this month, or last year to this year so I can see how my business has grown. For me, this can help keep me motivated and focused because I can see myself getting closer and closer to my ultimate goal.

Enjoy your journey as an author, and most of all, enjoy the freedom that comes from the extra income.

ABOUT THE AUTHOR

Jason has been writing books for several years, with many published on Amazon both under his name and a number of pseudonyms. He learned the craft by trial and error, making every mistake in the book and then some. Before this, he worked in the corporate world, being respectable and wearing a suit and tie every day. A large part of his existence was dedicated to writing tedious reports and technical documentation.

After his son was diagnosed with leukemia, he made the leap into being a full-time author as employers were unable to support his need for time off for hospital visits and treatment. Now his son has fully recovered, he writes full time and enjoys plenty of family time. With a passive income from his books, he can manage his own time, taking time off for days out as and when he wants.

His knowledge has been distilled into this book as he continues to develop his skills as a writer, cringes at his early books as he rewrites them and works to improve his marketing. Currently, he is building a large social media presence in preparation for approaching a traditional publisher for a forthcoming book.

In his spare time, he indulges his passion for gardening, growing a wide variety of fruits and vegetables, enjoying being outside.

You can find out more about Jason at his website, www.JasonEJohns.com or follow him on LinkedIn. He is on Twitter and Instagram as @allotmentowner if you want to see pictures of his plants.

www.ingramcontent.com/pod-product-compliance
Lightning Source LLC
Chambersburg PA
CBHW050907260726
48660CB00001B/73